The Prodigal System of Forgiveness and Reconciliation:

-=-

How to Heal from a Relational Crisis

J. Emmett Beam

Dedicated to…

Nancy Vu, Anh Nguyen and Sang Pham.

Words can not express all
that each of you mean to me.
You have enriched my life more
than anyone else. I love you!

CONTENTS

ACKNOWLEDGMENTS

First of all, I am most grateful to Jim Carroll for taking me through the forgiveness process for my own emotional healing in 1998 during one of his seminars. I thank both Jim and David Bishop for their friendship, for mentoring me as a director in the boot camps, and for training me to create and lead my own experiential workshops. If I had not experienced the power of forgiveness first hand, and been mentored and trained by Jim and David, I would not have been able to write this book about the process of forgiveness.

Thanks to my first copyeditor Susan Claunch who edited an early draft, believed in the value of the material and encouraged me to complete the book. Your confidence in the contents of the book is what convinced me to stay the course and complete the manuscript.

I can't say enough good things about Jarl Waggoner who did the final copyedit on the book. Jarl took my writing, which came in the form of reverse polish notation from me as a math major, and turned it into plain English readable by normal human beings. Thanks so much Jarl, you did a fabulous job.

Thanks to Sherry Stone for all the helpful suggestions in clarifying portions of the manuscript. Your insight and wisdom kept me on the right track.

My heartfelt thanks to Mary Moore, who spent so much time and ink on reviewing the book. Mary's thorough review was done with insight and skill. I appreciate Mary's persistence in wanting to have the book as theologically sound as possible. Mary, your attention to detail enhanced the quality of this book in so many ways. Thanks Mary!

Thanks so much to my good friend Bonnie Novak who started out as a reviewer, then used the book for her own healing and personal growth.

Thanks to Cynthia Martin Cook for putting the finishing touches on the book. Cindy is God's "go-to" person for getting things done. Thanks Cindy, your assistance was invaluable.

A big thanks to all the thousands of people who have attended one of the life enrichment boot camps, marriage boot camps, divorce recovery workshops or teen workshops featuring the forgiveness process. From their experience, the forgiveness process described in this book was honed and matured. Their healing not only validated the process, it's also the basis of healing for everyone who is healed by reading this book. Their pain is your gain.

I want to thank my parents John and Gladys Beam for always believing in me and for training me as a child in the way that I should go (Proverb 22:6)!

Emmett Beam

PREFACE

This book started out simply to be about forgiveness in human relationships. I've been conducting workshops since 1998 with "human forgiveness" as the central component. I have learned, practice and teach the skill of forgiveness. This book was simply going to be the result of writing down on paper what I know and teach. This book was going to be a short project and a piece of cake. After I read one short phrase in the Parable of the Prodigal Son everything changed. I realized that since this phrase was in the parable, I had to address it. So the focus expanded, and the book was no longer just a brain dump of the material I know intimately. What was that phrase? It was this: "Father, I have sinned against heaven." This one phrase in the parable expanded the focus to include a person's relationship with God. This expanded the spiritual dimension that is important to me personally. Now that the book is completed, I am thankful that it includes the additional material.

I believe this book is relevant for everyone. "To have life and to have it more abundantly" begins with a relationship with God. This abundance then spills over into all our relationships—personal, professional, and business.

The most important decision one makes in life is about his or her relationship with God. This book clearly shows how to start and maintain a relationship with God. Anyone who does not have a relationship with God can read this book and discover how easy it is to begin an eternal relationship with God and His Son, Jesus Christ. Everyone who has a relationship with God can benefit from knowing how to maintain fellowship with God. This book shows in very simple language how to do this.

Everyone wants friends and close, intimate relationships. But people hurt people, even the ones they love dearly. This book shows how to repair broken relationships. Not knowing how to repair broken relationships has dire consequences. Anyone who is angry at someone will end up being estranged from that person. Ultimately, the angry person is separated from everyone. One who does not learn how to forgive can end up a lonely old person. This book shows how to forgive and to reconcile relationships.

I hope this book brings you eternal joy and the most satisfying personal relationships for your entire life. Follow the principles described in this book and you can have everything you need and desire in this life, and the next one.

Blessings, Emmett Beam

INTRODUCTION

Life is about relationships. What makes life worth living is relationships. True riches are found in the relationships we make.
Money, possessions, and fame do not bring lasting happiness. They
may provide some comfort and freedom, but they do not bring inner
peace. Successful relationships don't just happen. It takes work
and skills to create, cultivate and maintain satisfying, fulfilling
relationships.

A relationship is a connection between two people. It takes both
people working together to make a relationship work. It takes only
one person to sour a relationship. One person's poor choices can
have an effect on many, many people, and the people hurt the most
are usually the people who are loved the most. So one person can
make one bad choice and cause a crisis in the lives of an untold
number of people—besides having a devastating effect on his own
life and career.

In the parable of the prodigal son the prodigal is typically identified as a rebellious teenage boy. In reality, a prodigal can be of
either gender, of any age, married or single. A personal crisis can
happen to anyone with devastating results on every relationship in
every area of the person's life. The personal crisis can destroy the
person's reputation, marriage, family, friendships, or partnerships.
The personal crisis can shame the person, his family, an organiza-
tion he represents, or even God.

A person does not just suddenly go bad. A person is just suddenly
found out. A person's character is suddenly revealed by his behavior.
Recently a minister of our church was arrested for soliciting sex

with a minor. He is fifty-two years old, a husband and father. The week he was arrested, the most common thing I heard from others members of our church was that "he was the last person I would think would do such a thing." His personality, his demeanor, his attitude, his effectiveness in performing his ministry duties, and his public relationship with his wife and son were all positive. His actions and behavior were always with integrity and unquestionable. His internal struggles were well hidden from everyone until the day he "acted them out" and was caught.

This has been a wake-up call for the members of our church. We all need to take a step back and examine ourselves. We have time to seek help with our internal struggles before we act them out. What can we learn from this man's failure? We should take an honest appraisal of ourselves and acknowledge to a trustworthy party our weaknesses and struggles. Then we should seek help from the appropriate professionals and support from a local support group.

If you're going through some very hard things right now and you are in extreme emotional pain, this book is probably not what you should be reading today. If you are in severe emotional pain, I suggest you contact your pastor, priest, rabbi, or professional counselor to help you in this time of crisis.

This book is designed to help you when you are in emotional rehab, not in the emotional emergency room. No book can take away the sting of suffering. Therefore, if you are currently in a difficult, painful crisis and in need of comfort and support, seek help from a crisis and trauma counselor or someone trained to help the grief stricken.

This book isn't meant to make you feel better by just skimming through it. To get the most out of this book, you will have to read and then reflect on what you just read and how it relates to your own life.

The purpose of this book is twofold. First, the spiritual purpose of this book is to present instructions on how to establish and maintain a relationship with God. Second, the relational purpose of this book is to teach you the process of forgiveness and reconciliation with other people. This process is referred to as *The Prodigal System of Forgiveness and Reconciliation.*

The book begins with two introductory chapters. The first defines parables and how they are used. The second describes a crisis and the stages of healing from a relational crisis.

Part 2 analyzes the parable of the prodigal son from various viewpoints, while part 3 looks at the theology of the parable.

The final section of the book deals with the healing of relationships as modeled by the parable of the prodigal son. Since the process of *The Prodigal System of Forgiveness and Reconciliation* is based on widely accepted principles, it is a model that can be used to heal from most relational crisis.

This book teaches practical skills built on spiritual truths. Biblical principles apply not only to a person's spiritual life but also to a person's daily emotional and psychological life. This book is meant to provide a solid basis for your effort to build and maintain a relationship with God and other people.

This book will challenge you to change. Skills necessary to excel in life are hard to learn, develop, and incorporate into our daily lives. Some skills are worth the time and effort. I believe the skills presented in this book, gleaned from the parable of the prodigal son, are the most important and necessary skills everyone needs to have in order to have a successful life.

Success in life is about relationships. This book will help you develop personal skills in having healthy relationships. Success in the next life is about having a relationship with God. This book will guide you through the process of creating and maintaining a personal relationship with God.

The Prodigal System of Forgiveness and Reconciliation is concerned about healing the whole person (except physical)—spiritual, emotional, and psychological.

- It deals with the spiritual part of man and his relationship with God.
- It deals with the social part of man and his relationship with other people.
- It deals with the emotional part of man and the effect of negative emotions on his attitudes and outlook on life and how these affect his relationship with God, himself, and others.

The research for the spiritual part is derived from a lifelong study of the Bible.

The Prodigal System of Forgiveness and Reconciliation presents how to establish a relationship with God. It also presents how to maintain fellowship with God after violating, or trespassing, one of God's laws or ordinances (sinning).

The Prodigal System of Forgiveness and Reconciliation presents the process of the healing of interpersonal relationships after a relational crisis (betrayal, abuse, crime, etc.).

The Prodigal System of Forgiveness and Reconciliation accomplishes the biblical instructions to establish and maintain a relationship with God, to forgive others when trespassed against, and to reconcile relationships when it depends on us.

A few people can forgive based on their spiritual belief and following the biblical principle of forgiveness. Most people find the forgiveness process extremely difficult. Most people cannot truly forgive from their heart until someone who knows how to forgive comes alongside them, and teaches them what true forgiveness is and demonstrates the process of forgiving. This book does exactly that. It shows how to heal from a relational crisis through forgiveness and reconciliation. Thousands have successfully used the principles described in this book.

PART ONE

INTRODUCTION

CHAPTER 1

Introduction to the Parable of the Prodigal Son

The Parable of the Prodigal Son in Luke 15 is one of the most popular and familiar stories in the Bible. The truths found in this parable are simple, yet very profound. Many people have said that this parable has had a more influential effect on their lives than any other parable in the Bible. The story is powerful and compelling. The message is clear. Families are going to go through times of crisis. Healing from a relational crisis is possible.

A parable is a short, fictitious narrative that illustrates a biblical principle. The Greek word for parable is parabole, a compound word comprised of the parts para, meaning "beside," and bole, meaning "to throw." The two parts together mean "to set alongside," meaning that "alongside" the fictional narrative is a set of biblical principles. The "throwing alongside of," or "placing alongside of," is for the purposes of comparison. A parable, therefore, places the truth to be taught alongside what is known and familiar. This is done in order to illustrate the essential truth of the principle being taught.

Jesus was a master at communicating to His audience by parable. The parables He told are as applicable to us today as they were to the people who lived two thousand years ago. This is especially true of the parable of the prodigal son. Families today still experience relational crises. The Parable of the Prodigal Son is a beautiful, exemplary story that presents a realistic, believable picture of a family going through a crisis.

Jesus used parables to convey spiritual truth in an easily understandable way. His parables took the familiar and applied it to the unfamiliar. In the parables Jesus used a lot of illustrations from common life. Through His use of similes, analogies, metaphors, and paradoxes, and through comparison or contrast, the unfamiliar was comprehended.

Mark 4:10-12 records, "As soon as He was alone, His followers, along with the twelve, began asking Him about the parables. And He was saying to them, 'To you has been given the mystery of the kingdom of God; but those who are outside get everything in parables, in order that while seeing, they may see and not perceive; and while hearing, they may hear and not understand lest they return and be forgiven.'"

By using parables Jesus also had the aim of concealing truth from those who lacked true spiritual interest. Parables still test the spiritual responsiveness of those who read them today. But anyone who is truly seeking to understand spiritual truths is given the keys to unlock his or her understanding to the truth behind a parable.

Since parables are analogies, this leads to personal interpretation of the parables by those who hear them. One author wrote that the common definition of a parable is "an earthly story with a heavenly meaning." I believe that any spiritual truth can have many practical applications in real life. The parables have spiritual meanings, but there are earthly applications of the spiritual truths taught in the parables.

The subject of this book is the Parable of the Prodigal Son. There are spiritual truths in this parable concerning human relationships. There are also spiritual truths about having a relationship with God. The people in the Parable of the Prodigal Son are representative of people and/or God, depending upon the interpretation.

There are literally thousands and thousands of published interpretations for the Parable of the Prodigal Son. This is the beauty of the parable. It contains many truths, and the truths have thousands of applications in the lives of all of us.

In this book there are interpretations for the Parable of the Prodigal Son for the different types of relationships we have. One interpretation is about family relationships, father to son and brother to brother. One interpretation is about starting a relationship with God. Another interpretation is about maintaining a relationship with God. And another interpretation is about religious and good people and their need for a relationship with God.

Representatives in the Parable

In one interpretation, the father in the parable represents God. The older son represents the scribes and Pharisees, who thought that salvation was a matter of meritorious works and outward piety. The younger son represents the rest of mankind, who acknowledge their sin and return to God for forgiveness. Since Jesus was speaking with the scribes and Pharisees when he told this parable, it makes sense that this is the most common interpretation.

In another interpretation, the father again represents God. However, the two sons represent two Christians who both struggle with carnality. The younger son represents the Christian who, after sinning, humbles himself, returns to God in the God-ordained way, and reestablishes his fellowship with God. The older son represents the Christian who does not deal with his sin and lives a carnal life.

In another interpretation, the father represents a real father who is a believer. The two sons represent two real teenage sons. The younger son represents a rebellious teenager who leaves home but later finds himself and returns home a changed person. The older son represents a self-righteous, jealous son who stays home but is spiritually dead; the parable does not indicate if he ever finds himself or not. For this interpretation, I prefer to call this story the "parable of the loving, forgiving father with two prodigal sons."

Each of these interpretations focuses on a specific application of a biblical truth. In this book these interpretations are explored, examined, and mined for principles that can enrich our spiritual lives and personal relationships.

The pattern of human behavior described in this parable is relevant for both the religious and non-religious person. Truth is valid and applies to everyone. Some Scriptures are directed only to believers, and some apply only to nonbelievers. Biblical truth about justice, integrity, forgiveness, and character is valid and applies to everyone.

This parable speaks to everyone about the universal process of having successful interpersonal relationships. The truth specifically referred to by the parable is the dynamic of receiving and giving forgiveness. Everyone who lives experiences to some degree hurt from other people. To heal our emotional wounds that result from that hurt, we all have to learn to forgive.

We all have within our internal belief system a process for when and how to forgive others for those emotional wounds resulting from previous offensive behavior. We also have in our internal belief system a process for when and how to forgive organizations, institutions, governments, government agencies, and religious organizations when we suffer injustices from their actions. We have in our internal belief system a process for when and how to forgive God if we believe He has failed us in some way. Even if someone doesn't believe in God, if he is angry at God, he has an emotional link to God that requires the use of forgiveness if he wants to be healed of that anger.

Therefore, every person needs to develop good skills in the act of giving forgiveness. Anyone can learn how to forgive by following the process of forgiveness presented in this book. Forgiveness is the most important skill for a person to learn, for it is the key to all successful relationships.

The other principles discerned from this parable are also important for a successful life. Most important are those that relate to the knowledge of God and our relationship with Him. Next are those that concern the knowledge of people and how we interact with other people. Next are principles of communication.

The behavior of a prodigal affects the life of the people around him or her. The prodigal's self-centered behavior creates a crisis in the life of the family. The healing process for the prodigal (the perpetrator), the originator of the crisis, is unique. The healing process for the family or victim(s) of the prodigal is different from the healing of the prodigal. Sometimes the people hurt by the actions of the prodigal prefer not to be called victims but people who have suffered unjustly or have been taken advantage of by the prodigal. The term victim is an all-inclusive term for those who suffer as a by-product of the rebellious, self-centered behavior of a prodigal.

The Parable of the Prodigal Son Taken from the Bible

Here is the parable of the prodigal son in its entirety from Luke 15:11-32 in the New American Standard Version.

11And He said, "A man had two sons.
12The younger of them said to his father, 'Father, give me the share of the estate that falls to me ' So he divided his wealth between them.
13"And not many days later, the younger son gathered everything together and went on a journey into a distant country, and there he squandered his estate with loose living.
14"Now when he had spent everything, a severe famine occurred in that country, and he began to be impoverished.
15"So he went and hired himself out to one of the citizens of that country, and he sent him into his fields to feed swine.
16"And he would have gladly filled his stomach with the pods that the swine were eating, and no one was giving anything to him.
17"But when he came to his senses, he said, 'How many of my father's hired men have more than enough bread, but I am dying here with hunger!
18'I will get up and go to my father, and will say to him, "Father, I have sinned against heaven, and in your sight;
19I am no longer worthy to be called your son; make me as one of your hired men."'
20"So he got up and came to his father. But while he was still a long way off, his father saw him and felt compassion for him, and ran and embraced him and kissed him.
21"And the son said to him, 'Father, I have sinned against heaven and in your sight; I am no longer worthy to be called your son.'

22"But the father said to his slaves, 'Quickly bring out the best robe and put it on him, and put a ring on his hand and sandals on his feet;

23and bring the fattened calf, kill it, and let us eat and celebrate;

24for this son of mine was dead and has come to life again; he was lost and has been found.' And they began to celebrate.

25"Now his older son was in the field, and when he came and approached the house, he heard music and dancing.

26"And he summoned one of the servants and began inquiring what these things could be.

27"And he said to him, 'Your brother has come, and your father has killed the fattened calf because he has received him back safe and sound.'

28"But he became angry and was not willing to go in; and his father came out and began pleading with him.

29"But he answered and said to his father, 'Look! For so many years I have been serving you and I have never neglected a command of yours; and yet you have never given me a young goat, so that I might celebrate with my friends;

30but when this son of yours came, who has devoured your wealth with prostitutes, you killed the fattened calf for him.'

31"And he said to him, 'Son, you have always been with me, and all that is mine is yours.

32'But we had to celebrate and rejoice, for this brother of yours was dead and has begun to live, and was lost and has been found.'"

CHAPTER 2

What Is a Relational Crisis?

The amazing thing about the Parable of the Prodigal Son is that almost everyone can point to some time in their life when his or her circumstances were similar to those described in the parable. The beauty of the parable is the innumerable ways in which people use it to analyze and interpret their circumstances, even though the people, places, and specific events may differ greatly. Over and over again, people experiencing a relational crisis can identify with one of the people in the parable.

Crises are of many different types. For one family, the crisis is dealing with a rebellious teenager. For another, it is the mid-life crisis of a husband trying to hang onto his youthfulness. And yet for another person, the crisis is the bitterness, anger, and frustration after the infidelity of a spouse. For some, the crisis is experiencing the hurt from an addiction of a spouse or other family member. For a teen, the crisis may be dealing with an emotionally or sexually abusive parent or step-parent. For a businessman, the crisis may be the possibility of facing bankruptcy after a business partner emptied the bank accounts and left the business. It may be the extended family experiencing guilt, shame, and introspection after a young family member is convicted of a sex offense.

A life crisis can have disastrous consequences for relationships. Some crises will terminate a long-term relationship. Some relationships will end because one person is so hurt and angry that he or she refuses to forgive the other person. Some relationships end because the perpetrator of an injustice does not choose to rebuild the relationship. Other relationships end because both people are too stubborn to make the first move toward reconciliation; they feel it would imply they were either wrong or weak. However, with determination and cooperation most relationships can be salvaged after a crisis.

A relational crisis does not have to end in disaster. Relationships can be rebuilt. Typically, when a relationship is rebuilt, there has been a life transformation for the prodigal and forgiveness on the part of the offended. The process of healing the relationships occurs in a predictable pattern and goes through several phases. The process of the reconciliation also follows the same phases.

Models of grief often are used to describe the phases or stages of grief. In The Phoenix Phenomenon by Joanne Jozefowski, five stages of grief are identified: impact, chaos, adaptation, equilibrium, and transformation. H. Norman Wright, in The New Guide to Crisis & Trauma Counseling, identifies four phases in the normal crisis pattern: impact, withdrawal/confusion, adjustment, and reconstruction/reconciliation. Wright's phases are based on Lloyd Ahlem's description in Living with Stress. In Gayle Reed's therapeutic model, "The Process of Forgiving Another," four phases are listed: uncovering, decision, work, and deepening/outcome.

The Gayle Reed Therapeutic Model

The Gayle Reed therapeutic model, given below, is one of the most thorough and complete models available today. The Reed model is an extrapolation from the therapeutic model and research produced at the University of Wisconsin-Madison by Robert Enright with the Human Development Study Group (1991, 1996, 2000).

Uncovering Phase

1. Examination of psychological defenses.
2. Confrontation of anger; the point is to release, not harbor the anger.
3. Admittance of shame, when this is appropriate.

4. Awareness of catharsis, energy depletion.
5. Awareness of cognitive rehearsal of the offense.
6. Insight that the injured party may be comparing self with the injurer.
7. Realization that one may be permanently and adversely changed by the injury.
8. Insight into a possibly altered "just world" view.

Decision Phase

9. A change of heart, conversion, new insights that old strategies are not working.
10. Willingness to consider forgiveness as an option.
11. Commitment to forgive the offender.

Work Phase

12. Reframing, through role-taking, the wrongdoer by viewing him or her in context.
13. Awareness of empathy and compassion toward the offender.
14. Acceptance, bearing, and grieving of the pain.
15. Giving moral gifts to the offender of mercy, generosity, and love.

Deepening/Outcome Phase

16. Finding meaning for self and others in the suffering and in the forgiveness process.
17. Realization that self has needed others' forgiveness in the past.
18. Insight that one is not alone (universality, support).
19. Realization that self may have a new purpose in life because of the injury.
20. Awareness of decreased negative affect and increased positive affect toward the offender. Awareness of internal emotional release.

Introduction to the Phases of Healing from a Relational Crisis

The following model, based on the above models, is used for this book. There are seven phases in a relational crisis.

The Story/Drama/Consequences Phase (Phase I)

Phase I is the story of the relationship. It lists the people in the parable and describes each person's relationship connection to the other people. It identifies the offensive behavior of one or more of the people and the reactions and behavior of the other people to the offensive behavior. As the drama of the story unfolds, it lists the feelings and attitudes of all involved. Finally, the suffering experienced, the consequences of the behavior of the offender, is noted.

Character weaknesses of the people involved are determined by their behaviors in the story. Some of the reasons for relational crises are that people can be selfish, rebellious, deceitful, self-centered, violent, abusive, negligent, sarcastic, insolent, negative, callous, disrespectful, unloving, unkind, and unappreciative, to name just a few. People also betray, ignore, or abuse someone they are in relationship with.

The Knowledge/Uncovering/Hope/Vision/Motivation Phase (Phase II)

Phase II begins when an offender start feeling the pain of the consequences of his choices and become introspective as to how he got into his current circumstances. He begins acknowledging his bad choices and taking responsibility for his actions. He stops blaming others as the cause of his misfortune. He begins to see that his choices were self-centered and that others have suffered because of his poor choices. He then begins to realize that if he changes his behavior, there is hope that life can be different for him. He sees the change he needs to make in order for the people in his life to accept him again and invite him back into their life. He becomes optimistic about making the inner changes, and therefore begins the process of changing his future.

If a person does not see any hope for change, he or she will become depressed and sink into deep hopelessness. When this occurs, irresponsible behaviors will continue; and the person will become angrier, more hostile, and, sometimes, even dangerously violent. When there is no hope, the person has no motivation to change his or her behavior.

This is the introspective phase for the offender. The uncovering occurs as the offender acknowledges his or her poor choices and assumes responsibility for those choices. The offender then lists his or her options. The offender then examines each option with a realistic view of the hope associated with the option. The offender then lists his or her desires and motivation to try this particular option. The key to the turnaround is finding hope in one or more of the options.

The Decision/Choices/Belief Phase (Phase III)

Phase III starts when the offender reviews all the choices and ultimately makes the decision of which option to take. The choices can be positive and responsible, or they can be negative and irresponsible. The choice could be to procrastinate and not make a choice at all. Hopefully the offender chooses the option he or she believes has the best chance of succeeding.

The desire for a better life and a positive attitude in knowing that it is possible motivates the offender to make the choices to change his behaviors in order to change his life. He may have felt guilty about how he has hurt others, and he is ashamed of himself for making the choices he did. In other words, he is now humble instead of arrogant and self-centered. He makes the decision to humble himself and to do whatever is required to start healing himself and rebuilding the relationships he has destroyed.

The Action/Change-of-Behavior Phase (Phase IV)

Phase IV begins when the person starts performing the actions and behaviors he or she had decided to undertake. It includes the actions actually made by the offender and the reactions of the others in the story. The actions are a change of behavior for the offender and reveal his or her brokenness and change of character.

The Deepening/Long-Term Proof/Wisdom-Maturity Phase (Phase V)

In phase V, when a person has a true change of heart, then the actions and behaviors begun in the previous stage will continue. This person will do everything necessary to regain trust. Such people do not mind being truthful and open about their activities and where they are at any point in time. They will be humble and appreciative of the acceptance and forgiveness of their spouses, family, friends, employers, and others whom they have hurt.

If the person did not have a change of heart, then the changes in behavior will be short-lived; and the person will return to his or her previous behaviors. People in this category are usually only sorry that they got caught and just want to be rescued from the consequences of their behaviors until they can regroup, restock, and replenish in preparation for their next adventure.

As the offender matures, he or she develops empathy for others and begins to show others love by helping them deal with similar problems that he or she overcame.

The Restitution Phase (Phase VI)

In phase VI restitution is occasionally a simple matter, but sometimes it is a very complicated process. When a crime is committed, the restitution is often set by the court system. Otherwise, the offended and the offender can attempt to resolve the issue of restitution. The offended states his expectations for restitution. The offender states his intentions for restitution. The two people negotiate a mutually agreeable settlement.

The Reconciliation Phase (Phase VII)

In phase VII, after a relational crisis and after the offended has forgiven the offender and the offender has made satisfactory restitution to the offended, the healing process moves to reconciliation. This is where both people involved decide to do all that is necessary to rebuild their relationship and friendship.

Forgiveness does not mean reconciliation. Either person in a conflict can prevent reconciliation. Not all relationships should be reconciled. If a person is still dangerous, threatening, or abusive, that person should not be allowed back into one's life.

Dan's Relational Crisis

Dan (not his real name) came to one of my workshops in the first quarter of 2002. His company was in the airline industry, and a recently canceled contract had left him a half-million dollars in debt. He was questioning himself and his abilities. He was angry, but not about his current circumstances. He was angry about something that had happened twenty years earlier. He told how twenty years ago a friend had introduced him to Tom (not his real name). Tom had been an employee of a large Christian ministry and was now looking for a job in the business world. Tom had connections in the oil business, and Dan was a computer hardware/software engineer. They formed a partnership on a handshake and began developing a system to automate the service station. After a year of nothing but development, all by Dan, and no income, they had a prototype working. Then one day, Tom disappeared. He moved to Houston and took most of the development equipment. Dan was left with most of the bills. Dan felt betrayed by Tom. As a Christian, Dan forgave Tom—so he thought. Somehow, the anger had resurfaced in Dan, and he was extremely angry at what Tom had done to him. Dan had forgiven from his head but not from his heart.

So I took Dan through the forgiveness process, and he forgave Tom from his heart. As soon as Dan finished, he said, "Now I can forgive my dad." I asked Dan what he meant because all weekend he had talked about how great his dad was and how good their relationship was. Dan told of how when he was fifteen his dad had divorced his mother and moved out of the country for ten years. Dan, a Boy Scout, did not complete his quest for becoming an Eagle Scout because his father was not there to help him. He felt betrayed by his father. But when his father came back into his life, he was so glad to have him back that he never mentioned the betrayal. Now Dan realized that he was holding anger, resentment, and bitterness against his dad. Dan forgive him right there on the spot. Those two betrayals had kept Dan from going into a partnership in the airline business several years ago. He tried to do it on his own and had made mistakes. Dan decided he would risk a partnership and see if he could save his company. And he did.

Dan's crisis included two betrayals decades apart. They left him in such fear that he made poor decisions, which cost him dearly. But he worked through his crisis, and life is going well for him still today.

Summary

This chapter describes the phases of healing from a relational crisis. Of course, people go through the process of healing in their own way and own time. There is no pattern that fits every person and all situations. Some people spend more time in one phase than they do in others. Some people bounce between the phases. Rarely does someone just go through the stages in a simple progression. Healing is complicated and usually involves some regression at times. The good news is that everyone can make it through the healing process, as the parable of the prodigal son illustrates.

PART TWO

ANALYSIS

CHAPTER 3

The Parable of the Prodigal Son as Two Unbelievers

Of his spiritual children, the apostle John wrote, "I have no greater joy than this, to hear of my children walking in the truth" (3 John 4). In contrast, it is equally true that there is nothing more painful for Christian parents than to see or hear of their children straying from the truth they were taught. Such parents certainly can identify with the father in Jesus' parable, but, more importantly, they can take hope from the Lord's story of a prodigal son.

In this chapter the parable of the prodigal son is examined from the interpretation of the father being a devout Christian and his two sons both being unbelievers at the beginning of the parable. The first part of this parable deals with the family crisis caused by the rebellious nature of the younger brother (vv. 11-24). The last part deals with the family crisis caused by the rebellious nature of the older brother (vv. 25-32).

This chapter demonstrates how to do the analysis in the knowledge/uncovering phase of the healing process. I examine the parable for information revealed about each person in the parable. Since behavior tends to reveal what people are thinking and feeling, the behaviors of each person in the parable are examined for important pieces of information about the person. Some of the information from the story is obvious. Other information I have gleaned by using my imagination as I placed myself directly into the story. Some information about the story or people I have discerned by "reading between the lines."

Sometimes what is not said is just as meaningful as what is said in the parable, so I'll be raising questions that are not explicitly answered in the parable. If these questions were answered in the parable, it would be much easier to see the purpose of the parable. But parables are designed to function like puzzles that require contemplation and analysis in order to ascertain the meaning.

Listening is an important skill and also one of the hardest communication skills to learn. As you read the analysis below, see if you can determine how I "heard" what I did from reading the verses. Mark things that you question about my interpretation and come back later when you've finished the book to see if you still question them. When you discern things that I didn't mention, write them in the margin of the book for later review.

Verse-by-Verse Analysis

Luke 15:11 And He said, "A man had two sons.

What we know from this verse is that the man has two sons. We don't know whether his wife is still living or not. We don't know the background of the father. We don't know about the relationship the father has with either of his sons. We don't know about the relationship between the two sons.

We do learn several things about the father. He was a man of faith, and he taught his family spiritual values. He trained his children in the way they should go. He was the example to his family. He was a man of integrity. He had a relationship with God. He lived his faith. He trusted God. He waited on God. He was a man of prayer. He knew his children and their personalities. He loved his family. He loved both his sons equally.

12 "The younger of them said to his father, 'Father, give me the share of the estate that falls to me.' So he divided his wealth between them.

The younger son wanted his inheritance. The younger son said, "Give me." The younger son wanted his inheritance NOW.

The younger son appears to be proud, unthankful, ungrateful, wayward, irreverent, uncontrolled, indulgent, strong-willed, deceitful, egocentric, self-centered, and self-seeking. The younger son most likely had been aggressive all his life. Everyone would know that he was aggressive, as they would have observed this as part of his personality.

The younger son is put off by his submissive brother. He can't see himself playing second fiddle to someone who has no motivation or goals and is a people pleaser.

The younger son is confident, but his confidence in himself leads him to be prideful, self-sufficient, and independent. This self-centered pride had him thinking that he was capable enough to make it on his own without his family and without God.

The survival of the fittest motivates the younger son to leave the safety of his home and family. The younger son also knows that if he remains at home and works hard and is successful, he will get only half as much as his brother. The younger son knows that if he works harder and smarter than his older brother, he will not be rewarded for it. He could "outwit, outplay, and outlast" his brother, and there would be no reward for it because his share of the inheritance would stay the same. Maybe he felt his older brother was just a follower and not a leader, or maybe he believed his older brother was lazy.

- What freedom did the younger son need that was being limited by staying home?
- Did he feel guilty for having to take control of the family business and make it go when his lazy older brother should have been in charge, overseeing the whole family business?
- Was the younger son ashamed of how he was treating his brother?

The younger son acknowledges that his inheritance is free to him, something he has not earned. This reminds us of an important principle: We don't value anything we don't work for and earn.

A person's behavior reveals what is in his heart. For instance, a statement a person makes when drunk is a statement the person thought of before, when he or she was sober. A person does not just suddenly go bad; he or she is just suddenly found out. Eventually the masks come off, and people reveal their true nature.

The father showed respect for the younger son by respecting his personal space, honoring his physical territory, honoring his possessions, and allowing him to be his own person. The father allowed the younger son to chart his own path. The father did not try to make the younger son follow in his own footsteps.

The father maintained a healthy personal relationship with his younger son by not violating the younger son's physical, emotional, spiritual, or values "space." Even though the father did not necessarily agree with his younger son's choices, the father respected his decisions and allowed him to be separate and unique. The father knew what not to do; so he never intruded. The father did not want his younger son to become defensive and vigorously defend himself and his "space."

- Did the father feel responsible for the younger son's choice?
- Is this the reason the father gave to the younger son the money for his inheritance early?

The father had a decision to make when the younger son asked for his share of the inheritance. The father chose to divide to both of his sons their inheritance from his living. His living, or wealth, means his business. This is how the father supported himself and his family. The father knew that his business would suffer from losing access to those assets.

The father did not have the need for self-protection or control. He lost part of his business when he gave control of it to the younger son. The younger son inherited one-third of the family assets. This was the customary amount. Of course it could have been different, but since the father was just, he probably followed the society custom at the time.

- Did the younger son feel inferior to the older son or his father?
- Did the younger son feel embarrassed over something about himself?

Unhealthy shame drives one away from others and eventually causes one to turn against himself. Healthy shame is a personal, moral, and emotional smoke detector that forewarns one of danger, and prevents one from entering potentially dangerous personal situations.

- Was shame somehow involved in the younger son's decision to leave?
- What kind of resistance was the younger son getting at home because of his aggressiveness?
- Did the younger son have problems with his father? Brother? Servants?

13a "And not many days later, the younger son gathered everything together and went on a journey into a distant country,

A few days after receiving his inheritance, the younger son gathered all his possessions and money and went on a trip into a far country. The younger son was being controlled by his emotions: pleasure and lust.

The older brother did not try to stop him, most likely because of jealousy. The older brother was probably glad to see his younger brother leave despite the loss of the money, the property, and his brother's help in the family business.

The father knew he could not reason with the younger son, so he did not try to change his younger son's mind about leaving.

The father began praying for his son, for his protection and specifically in regard to his salvation. The father now had no control or influence over his son. But the father did have power with God. He put his faith in God to answer his prayers about his son. He knew he had brought up his son in the proper manner. He had taught his son about God. He had been the proper example. He knew he had no choice but to give his son over to God and depend on Him to bring his son back safely.

The younger son was assertive and maybe even a little aggressive. He would seek to get his own needs met at the expense of others. He was being rebellious. He wanted to have control over his own life. He wanted to live the unrestrained life and make all his own choices.

The younger son had confidence in his own ability to succeed at everything he attempted to do. He was used to being praised for his accomplishments.

The younger son was at the point in his life when he wanted to experience pleasure. He was tempted and deceived by the lure of pleasure and the lust of the flesh. The younger son was going through a period of willful disobedience. This, combined with his desire for pleasure, led him to make shortsighted decisions about his life.

The younger son did not have a weak ego. He was not boastful, overbearing, or dominating in his assertiveness or his aggressiveness.

- Was there pain at home that the younger son was trying to escape?
- Was the younger son overwhelmed at home and trying to cope with living by leaving?
- Why did he go to a far country instead of staying close by in his own country?
- What was the younger son trying to avoid?
- What did the younger son think he could gain?
- What drew him to that far country?
- What kind of people did he run into in the far country?
- What need inside of him was he trying to meet?
- Was the younger son seeking a mood-altering experience to escape the pain of life?
- Was he medicating the pains of life by relying on this behavior?

- Did he feel better when he was giving in to his addiction of loose living?
- Which part of this made him feel better or altered his mood?
- Was he doing this to make friends or for personal pleasure?
- Did he believe that by spending all he had in loose living with his new friends that they were obligated to give back to him at some later time?

13b and there he squandered his estate with loose living.

The younger son wasted his possessions and money on riotous living. He chose to spend his money in this way, and he spent it all.

In this behavior, the younger son was not codependent and trying to rescue people, so he would not have felt "used" by his new friends.

- Why wasn't he thinking of the future?
- What led him to believe he did not need to save for a rainy day?
- Why did he not invest part of the money?
- Did the younger son violate previously held morals or boundaries?
- Was living this way an offense to his conscience?
- Did the younger son feel guilt or self-condemnation?
- How did he look at the consequences of his actions?
- Did he think he would avoid the consequences with help of his new friends?

The word prodigal means "debased," or "extravagant." How was the younger son's style of living both debased and extravagant?

14 "Now when he had spent everything, a severe famine occurred in that country, and he began to be impoverished.

Famine is part of life. Life in this world is unpredictable and can involve unfortunate things like famine, failure, loss, struggles, disappointment, bad timing, pain, sorrow, disease, and death. No one is exempt from the unpredictability of life.

Everyone in that country was affected by the famine. There was a shortage of food, and there were no jobs available. The younger son was in serious trouble because he had no money for food or lodging, and he had no job.

- Did he feel angry, resentful, bitter, or frustrated with his new friends?
- Did the younger son feel angry or frustrated with himself?

15 "So he went and hired himself out to one of the citizens of that country, and he sent him into his fields to feed swine.
16 "And he would have gladly filled his stomach with the pods that the swine were eating, and no one was giving anything to him.

Even in the famine, the younger son was ambitious and confident enough to go and find a job. He took a job with a local citizen of that country. He did not care what kind of job he took; he would accept anything in order to have food and lodging.

The younger son had a good work ethic, and because of this, he managed to immediately get a job to meet his needs. His father had taught him this good work ethic.

The young man's boss sent him to feed swine. He was sent out there alone to do a menial, unskilled, and unfulfilling job, but he had the inner strength to go and do the job he was hired to do.

The younger son's work regimen was very physical. This exercise would raise his spirits by increasing the level of endorphins, which are brain chemicals that act as a natural pain reliever. These endorphins may have also helped him feel better emotionally.

The younger son was out in the field alone and completely isolated from everyone. Yet, he did not blame others for his circumstances. No doubt his father taught him not to blame others for self-inflicted misery. The young man accepted the consequences of his bad choices.

No one came to see him. No one with whom he had wasted his money came to visit him or offer any assistance. The younger son soon became sick from feeding swine and longing for their food.

As soon as his physical health began to decline, he knew he had to do something. It was a mental decision. He "came to himself."

- He felt lonely.
- He missed having good food.
- He missed his father and his life at home.
- He missed responsibility.
- He missed the luxury of having servants.
- He missed his brother.
- He missed his job.
- He missed being a boss.
- He despised working with swine.
- He despised being sick from malnutrition.
- He despised being alone.

The younger son may have felt guilt over not honoring his father, hurting his father's business by taking resources from it, and hurting his brother by not doing his share of the work. The younger son may have felt a little shame over being humiliated by working with swine, not having the character and integrity of his father, and not behaving in a way that was consistent with how he was raised.

He knew he had caused these painful events to occur in his life. He examined his circumstances, and he did not like them. He did not like what he did to himself. He was the one who got himself into this mess.

But what were his options? Getting another job probably would not happen. He knew the servants back home had it better than he did.

- Did he feel sorry for himself?
- What self-preservation instinct warned him, or got his attention, so that he went into action to correct his circumstances?

He knew he had to take care of himself. His father had taught him this. He never felt powerlessness, deep shame, self-loathing, self-hatred, terror, or desperation when examining his situation. His emotions were not his enemies, and they were not controlling him. He was not depressed. He did not feel low, did not lose interest in living, did not change his behavior, did not cry, did not lack motivation, did not lose his appetite, did not get fatigued, did not lose concentration, and did not become pessimistic.

He may have been depressed a little, but he wasn't paralyzed by it. In fact, it would have motivated him to take action to get out of his mess.

It is strange the young man was not extremely depressed since he had a great financial loss. He lost his father and brother when he separated from them. He lost his direction in life. He lost his job. He did not have friends. He had moved to a new location. He had lots of stress. He had financial difficulties. He had long, bad work hours at a poor location. He had pressure to make sure he kept his job. He had no counselor or anyone to talk to. Things were getting worse. He lost his health and vitality.

He was fulfilling his responsibilities at his job. He did the work he was supposed to do and did not take advantage of his boss. He did not expect anyone to rescue him. He worked in order to get by. Even during this time, he was emotionally healthy enough to accept full responsibility for his life.

He did not have a martyr's attitude of saying, "I deserve to be miserable." His father taught him better than to think these kinds of thoughts. His father had taught him to never give up. He was not angry at his father for giving him the money to leave. He was not ungrateful for what he had. He saw the glass as half full and not half empty. He kept a good perspective about himself. He had a healthy view of life, realizing that "we reap what we sow."

17 "But when he came to his senses, he said, 'How many of my father's hired men have more than enough bread, but I am dying here with hunger!

The young man realized that he had to do something or this was going to kill him. It was then that he came to himself. He found the answer. He realized that he had to take responsibility to change his life. He had to take action to rescue himself from the consequences of his own bad behavior. He was thinking of his options. Here is an important principle: Until you confront the problems, there can be no solutions.

The prodigal acknowledged his pain: he was extremely hungry. He came to himself. He reached bottom, and he came to his senses. He acknowledged that he had made some bad decisions, and he forgave himself for making the bad choices. He was repentant, broken. He was willing to deal with the issues and rearrange his life. He made the decision to do something about it. He decided to get control of his life again, and he developed a plan regarding what he was going to do to solve his current problems.

18 'I will get up and go to my father, and will say to him, "Father, I have sinned against heaven, and in your sight;

The young man decided he was immediately going to implement the plan to regain control of his life. His losses turned his focus back to God. Maybe it was a spiritual awakening for him. It took the focus off of self and put it back on God, for just out of the blue, the younger son declared his behavior to be a sin against God. Simply put, the verb "to sin" means to do something contrary to God's will. All sin, therefore, is, first and foremost, sin against God. This implies that the younger son had been taught values and spiritual principles by his father.

He acknowledged the fact that he had sinned by his behavior. He acknowledged he had broken at least one of the Ten Commandments because his behavior did not honor his father and mother. He was not in denial about his sin.

The younger son determined to go to his father. He would tell his father he had sinned against God and against his father. He was willing to admit that he had made a mistake, just as his father had taught him to acknowledge his mistakes and learn from them.

He was not fearful of going to his father. He knew his father would listen to him. His father did not have rules that would prevent him from expressing his feelings, thoughts, opinions, desires, or perceptions. His father was open to helping others and merciful to those in need.

He knew his father was not controlling since his father had given him his inheritance. He knew his father had confidence in God, for he had surrendered one-third of his business but had faith that God would meet his needs.

The younger son knew his father lived by integrity, values, and morals. His father was well respected in the community and was a good businessman, never wasting money. He knew he did not measure up to his father's character. He could see himself missing the mark of having integrity. He had missed the mark of the glory of his father.

- Did he feel sad or disappointed in himself? Was there self-hatred?
- Did he do anything that says he condemned himself for doing what he did?
- Was he troubled about who he was now?
- Was he defining himself by his past behavior?
- Should he have felt ashamed or guilty?

The young man was going to admit that he had sinned against God. His father had taught him to confess his sin, not hide it. His father had taught him that God has unconditional love, grace, and mercy and is willing to forgive and cleanse us from our sin. His father had taught him that his standing with God was dependent on God and his grace, His unmerited favor, and not on his behavior, outward appearance, worldly status, or wealth.

Obviously his father had taught him spiritual principles. The younger son knew how to handle spiritual guilt. He accepted responsibility for having violated the moral boundaries of his father by asking to be made a servant (v. 19).

The younger son also was going to acknowledge his sin against his father. He was showing he knew how to handle personal guilt by acknowledging the transgressions to his father.

His father obviously had taught him to admit his mistakes when he did something wrong. His father had taught him how to ask for forgiveness by acknowledging wrongdoing.

The younger son was determined to make amends by being a good worker for his father. He was going to make up for all the inconvenience and pain he had caused his father and family. He knew his behavior had hurt others, and he was willing to accept responsibility for those bad decisions and make amends. His actions would demonstrate that he was truly sorry for the pain he had caused.

The younger son was not ashamed of himself. He had been taught better than to feel that way. His father taught him to never feel shame and how to handle appropriately legitimate guilt. He was not afraid to admit his human weaknesses.

Certain feelings and behaviors can be observed in people who feel shame. They:

- feel inadequate
- hide and avoid people
- distance themselves from God
- feel sad, fearful, self-loathing and troubled by who they are
- pretend to be something other than what they are
- exaggerate about themselves, brag, name-drop
- assume blame when treated badly
- are unable to accept themselves
- keep secrets about themselves
- lose themselves in the needs of others
- defy societal norms,
- fear expressing their opinion
- become perfectionists
- fear failure
- are unable to ask for help
- resist setting goals

- feel permanently flawed
- feel that something is wrong with them.

The younger son was not gripped by shame.

19 I am no longer worthy to be called your son; make me as one of your hired men.'"

The prodigal decided to return home, admit his mistakes to his father, and humble himself and work as a hired hand for his father. The younger son knew his father as a person with character and saw himself as lacking the same character as his father.

He was showing remorse by saying that he was not worthy to be called his father's son. He was sorry and remorseful over not measuring up to the character of his father. He knew he fell short of the glory of his father. He acknowledged his humbleness by saying he was not worthy of being referred to as his father's son. He acknowledged his father as righteous and as a person who makes good decisions. He acknowledged that he was not righteous like his father. His behavior hurt how he viewed himself and how he felt others would view him.

The younger son was willing to accept and suffer the consequences of his bad choices. He had no expectations; he was humble and realistic.

20a "So he got up and came to his father.

The younger son followed his plan. He started the journey home the next day when he got out of bed. He kept traveling until he arrived back home.

He knew his father would forgive him. His father had taught him to forgive, and he had seen his father forgive others. He knew his father was a forgiving person and it was safe to return to his father.

The younger son did not procrastinate. He did not put off the important task of addressing this issue. Fear did not rule his life so that he looked for reasons to put off leaving. He was emotionally able to face his father without any hesitation. He knew the benefits of going home to his father. He knew this decision to go home was right. It was the highest priority in his life. It was the most important thing for him to do in order to point his life in a new direction. He was confident about his ability to accomplish this goal. He did not delay his journey home by going to his boss and saying good-bye. He got up early the next morning and left for home.

20b But while he was still a long way off, his father saw him and felt compassion for him, and ran and embraced him and kissed him.

The father was expecting his younger son to return. He was constantly watching the road for any sign of his son coming home. He prayed every day and knew that one day God would answer his prayer. He looked expectantly every day that it might be that day when God answered his prayer. One day, as the father was watching for his younger son, he spotted him a long way off.

The father felt compassion for his son.

- Was it his body language?
- Was it that the father knew that he must have hit bottom for him to be returning home?
- Was it that the son had no provisions with him and his father knew that he must have lost everything?
- Could his father see that he was sick from malnutrition?
- Was the son walking differently?
- Was he thin?
- Did other parts of his demeanor or maybe his clothes or his hair incite his father's compassion?

The father ran to his son immediately. Obviously the father already had forgiven him. It is no surprise to us that the father welcomed his son with an embrace and a hug.

21 "And the son said to him, 'Father, I have sinned against heaven and in your sight; I am no longer worthy to be called your son.'

The younger son acknowledged to his father his sin against God and God's moral laws. He acknowledged his sin against his father. He acknowledged that he did not have the same integrity as his father and was not worthy to be called his son. He acknowledged a difference in character. He knew he had shamed the family before the community, which had in the past had such respect for his father. He knew he did not measure up to the glory of his father.

The younger son gave the heartfelt "confession of a sinner." He acknowledged that he deserved punishment, that he expected nothing, and that he was relying on mercy from his father. He was expressing his remorse for not measuring up to the standards set by his father.

The father listened to what his younger son said, and then the father interrupted him before he could finish what he had prepared to say to his father.

22 "But the father said to his slaves, 'Quickly bring out the best robe and put it on him, and put a ring on his hand and sandals on his feet;

"But" points out the father's assertiveness. The father himself took charge of the moment and directed everyone as to what to do now that his younger son was back.

The father addressed his comments to the servants, not his younger son. He did not try to reason with his son and tell him not to feel that way about himself. The father knew actions speak louder than words. The actions of the father said more to the younger son than anything the father could have said.

The father was in control and let everyone know his feeling toward his son, how he was going to treat his son, and how he wanted everyone else to treat his younger son. The father told the servants what he wanted done for his younger son. The father let everyone know how he felt about his son. He had forgiven and pardoned him. The father also was going to take care of his son's emotional needs. The father was declaring that he could once again enjoy the privileges he had forfeited when he had asked for his inheritance and left home.

Then, as a good administrator of his servants, the father delegated the tasks to be done.

23 and bring the fattened calf, kill it, and let us eat and celebrate;

The father told the servants to prepare the food for a feast. The importance of this occasion is established by the killing of the special calf that was reserved only for the most important occasion. The father let the servants know that this was a time for everyone to celebrate the return of the younger son. The father said, "Let us," which is inclusive of everyone in the family, including the servants, to be happy about the return of the son. It was a time for everyone to stop working, rejoice, and have the best food and best celebration.

The father was generous and thoughtful, kind, and considerate of the feelings of others. The father treated his servants with great respect.

The father knew that relationships are the most important things in life. He knew that a ceremony was necessary to mark this occasion and show the importance of having his "new" son back.

Confession of sin brought full restoration to the younger son.

24 for this son of mine was dead and has come to life again; he was lost and has been found.' And they began to celebrate.

The father told his servants that his younger son had been dead and was now alive, that the younger son had been lost but was now found. The father did not deny the truth that his younger son had been rebellious and behaved selfishly. After the father toasted the reason for the party, the celebrating began.

The father knew that his younger son was dead and lost even before he left home with his inheritance. He knew the condition of his younger son.

The father did not say he was glad his assertive son was back, that his hard working son was back, that the son he could bounce things off of was back. What was important to the father was that his younger son was now alive. He was glad his son had a change of character, a change of heart. This change in his younger son's heart was what they were celebrating.

The younger son actually received salvation. He acknowledged his sin. He acknowledged he did not measure up to his father's standard, let alone the glory of God. He acknowledged that he deserved punishment for his sin. He acknowledged that he was a sinner and did not measure up and therefore needed a savior.

Note that the father was able to express his feelings. He was in charge of his life. The father knew when to work, when not to work, and when to celebrate. The father knew the significance of this event in the life of his family. It is an important one-time occurrence when someone comes to life again. When someone makes the most important decision in life, it must be celebrated.

The joy was back in the father's heart, and he wanted to share that joy with everyone else.

> **25 "Now his older son was in the field, and when he came and approached the house, he heard music and dancing.**
> **26 "And he summoned one of the servants and began inquiring what these things could be.**
> **27 "And he said to him, 'Your brother has come, and your father has killed the fattened calf because he has received him back safe and sound.'**

The older son could hear the festivities from a distance and called a servant to find out why the music and dancing was going on at his home. The older son was clueless as to any reason that would justify such activity at his home.

The older son was not expecting his younger brother to return home. He also was not expecting his father to throw a huge celebration for his younger brother since the younger brother had left home with his inheritance and hurt the family business.

- Why did the servant not come to him on his own and tell him what was going on?

- Did the servants know that the older son would not be happy about what was transpiring?
- Why did the servant only of speak of "safe and sound" when the father had spoken of the son being alive and found?"

It seems the servants did not fully understand why the celebration was being held because they did not know about the change that occurred in the heart of the younger son.

28a "But he became angry and was not willing to go in;

The older son was selfish and jealous, and he decided not go in and be part of the celebration. The older son was legalistic, self-righteous and angry. He had no love and no mercy.

However, the older son was submissive. He was sacrificing himself for his father and the family business. But when someone sacrifices and gives and doesn't receive back, then resentment builds in that individual's heart if the person has been sacrificing and giving for the wrong reasons.

The party and the celebration were too much for the older son. He felt it was not fair. He was here and did everything his father asked, but he was never given a party. Now his younger brother had returned after wasting their resources, and his father was giving this rebellious brother of his a party. The reality of this was just too much for the older son.

The opportunity to be rewarded with a feast and party was now gone for the older brother, for it was wasted on his worthless younger brother. The older son felt he, not his younger brother, deserved the accolades of his father.

The older son had handled his emotions for all these years, but now he could not do it any longer. The older son could no longer be submissive emotionally. He reached the boiling point. The older son expressed his pent-up emotions and anger at his father by refusing to attend the celebration.

What a tragedy it was for the older brother to not want to go see his younger brother, who had been gone for so long. The older brother was missing an opportunity to re-connect with his long-lost younger brother. This shows that the older son had little or no compassion.

The older brother isolated himself. He wanted to ruin the good time his brother was having by throwing a wet rag on the party and celebration. He was giving his younger brother the silent treatment.

The older brother did not care what the consequences were for not connecting and reuniting with his younger brother. The older brother's response was not appropriate for the situation.

- Was the older son wanting others to feel sorry for him and come console him?
- What were all these repressed emotions doing to the older son physically and mentally?
- Had the older son always been jealous of his younger brother?
- Was the older brother really the weaker of the two brothers?
- Did the older brother resent being controlled by his younger brother?
- Was the older brother insecure?

The older brother was alienated from his aggressive brother because of his younger brother's behavior. His younger brother was aggressive, and he was submissive. The two brothers were total opposites.

28b and his father came out and began pleading with him.

James 1:20 warns us that **"the anger of man does not achieve the righteousness of God."** The father knew his older son was angry and would not go in, but he did not shy away from this encounter with his older son. The father went out immediately and engaged his older son in order to end this conflict in a constructive manner.

The father did not send a servant with an order for his son to attend the feast. The father did not send a servant to tell the older son that his father wanted to meet with him to discuss the matter. The father himself went, and went alone, in order to deal with the anger of his older son. His younger son was changed. Now he had to focus on his older son.

The father knew that this conflict needed to be faced and resolved at the earliest possible moment. The father knew he had to intervene with his submissive, angry older son. He had to address the fears of his older son. He had to let him know how much he was loved and how much his father wanted him to make the right decision also.

There is no affection shown here between the father and his oldest son. The father simply entreated his son. The father did not sternly tell his older son he better come to the celebration or face some consequences. The father did not coerce his older son to come to the festivities. Rather, he reasoned with his older son and put forward a humble plea and appeal for him to come. The father was almost begging for his older son to come see his younger brother and join in the festivities.

The father responded with sensitivity toward his older son. He cared about how his older son was feeling, so he went to him immediately and reasoned with him.

The father did not have anxiety and fears about approaching his son. He was not trying to control his older son or run his son's life. He reasoned with him; he did not attempt to manipulate his son with guilt. He did not attack his son and cause his son to raise his defenses.

The father was not seeking power or trying to save face. He loved his older son and wanted him to respond properly to the situation.

The father knew that his older son was still dead and lost, so he was going to do everything possible to help his older son be found and come alive. He left the living son and went to the dead son. He knew his dead son needed his attention, so he left the celebration to take care of his dead and lost son.

Undoubtedly, the father asked his son some questions: "What has upset you so much that you have not come to the celebration?" "I would like to know how you view what is happening. How do you feel about this?" Such questions do not focus on behavior but on feelings. They are an invitation to open up. The father expressed concern about the older son and demonstrated his acceptance of him.

The father did not attack the behavior or character of his oldest son; he did not put him down or angrily denounce him. The father treated his older son with respect. He was really trying to help his older son by going to him and urging him to do the right thing.

29a "But he answered and said to his father, 'Look! For so many years I have been serving you and I have never neglected a command of yours;

The older son let out an angry outburst of his thoughts and feelings to his father. With this outburst the older son finally verbalized what he had thought and felt for years. The father had talked to the older son in a way that encouraged his son to be genuine and direct in expressing his feelings about what he was angry about. The father did this well because the older son thoroughly vented his feelings and discharged his heightened emotion. This allowed them to discuss their differences in a productive manner.

Conflict is unpredictable. The older son had to be unsure of what was going to happen when his father first appeared. This had to have increased his emotional uneasiness. He was not accustomed to choosing the "fight" stance when in a conflict situation. Undoubtedly, he usually backed down and became passive and chose "flight" to avoid confrontation.

For the first time the older son showed disrespect to his father. In the past he had always wanted to be seen in a positive light by his father. He had always said "yes" to his father, but he was thinking "no" in his heart.

In that society children were taught unquestioned obedience. The father was the patriarch until his death. But children were allowed to voice their opinions. Fears kept the older son from expressing himself, even when it would benefit the family. The older son had an unhealthy relationship with his father. He was afraid of rejection. He always said "yes" out of his fear that it was the only way for him to stay in everyone's good graces. To him the only way to be accepted was to do what others wanted him to do all the time.

The older son always hid his feeling from his father. The older son based his self-esteem and worth on the basis of what he did for his father. If he had refused to do something, his value would have diminished. He felt better about himself because he was pleasing other people. He pretended everything was fine. He could not deal with reality. He was a "yes" man. He was afraid to be himself. He felt if he were himself he would be rejected.

The older son had uncomfortable, embarrassing thoughts and kept them hidden. He did the opposite of his thoughts and urges and portrayed himself as an overly moral and righteous person. He became preoccupied with being a good moral, dependable person in order to avoid the anxieties of his compulsive immoral urges.

The older son claimed that he was compliant, obedient and had surrendered his will to the conditions imposed on him by his father. His compliance was not true submissiveness, however, which is humble cooperation and meekness.

For years this son had been trying to get his father's approval by his actions. Not getting it has led to resentment and anger building up in him. He had been in denial and pretending that everything was all right between him and his father. In the past he always had withdrawn and avoided the situation when asked to do something that he did not desire to do. He built a falsely peaceful façade and acted like nothing ever upset him. He always capitulated, gave in to his father's wishes, and never had his own needs met. This fear of confrontation resulted in submissive and passive behavior, and his avoidance of confrontation resulted in a distant and shallow relationship with his father.

It is not out of reason to think that the older brother, because of his position and outward submission to his father, was very dominant and aggressive toward his younger brother. The older brother may have dominated his younger brother because the older was given the authority by his father, not because the older son was the stronger or more capable person. This could have led to resentment by the younger brother. Since there was no peace, joy, or delight in working with the older brother, the younger brother fought back by asking for his share of his inheritance and leaving the family and family business and his older brother's domination.

- What were the older son's fears? What intimidated him?
- Why did he not voice his opinion before this?
- Why did he explain himself now and not sooner?
- Why could he not make decisions or choices?
- Did he not have confidence in his decision-making process?
- Did he feel incapable of assuming authority?
- Was he afraid that he would fail?
- Did he feel like he was fooling his father all these years?
- Why could he not confide in his father? Did he not trust his father?

All these years he had been a nice son. He was quiet and obedient. He went along with everything his father asked him to do. He never complained or questioned anything, because he felt he had to "go along" with the wishes of his dad.

His exterior of being a "nice child" was only a façade covering a sordid interior. His exterior attitude of being "nice" was not what he was feeling in his heart. His resentment was growing each day that he had to pretend to be enjoying his life working for his father. The older son did not have a life. He was not really living. He had friends, but they were more like companions.

Just like his younger brother, the older son did not have a spiritual life. The father was wise in allowing his sons to begin to seek a spiritual life on their own time frame. Anything forced on one is eventually resented. Learning obedience to our earthly father is training to obey God, our heavenly Father. Choosing to obey is different from being forced to obey or obeying for inappropriate reasons.

Submissive people repress their negative emotions. But the negative emotions and thoughts are usually acted out in passive-aggressive ways. The father knew when his son was being passive-aggressive in his behavior.

The older son never ventured out and tested the boundaries with his father. He just went along. He was squandering his life by kowtowing to the desires and commands of his father.

The older son was not close to his father. The relationship was not satisfying for either one of them. The older son never asked for anything for himself. He took what was offered to him. He forfeited himself and his life by molding himself into the picture he had in his mind of what was lovable to his father. He felt his father wanted obedience. He was not real with his father.

In anger the older son finally expressed his thoughts and feelings. This outburst reveals that he did not have an intimate relationship with his father. Intimacy has been characterized as "the ability to express one's hopes, dreams, deepest aspirations, fear, anxieties, feelings of guilt, and areas of shame with another significant person repeatedly." The older son did not have this type of relationship with his father.

The wise father recognized that his older son was not able to express his deepest thoughts and feelings because he was insecure and fearful. The father could see that he was leading a life full of anxiety and avoidance.

The older son finally did something that was not submissive. But he went to the other extreme with an aggressive outburst of anger, resentment, bitterness, and sarcasm. The pressure inside of him reached the explosive boiling point, and he unleashed his emotions on his father.

29b and yet you have never given me a young goat, so that I might celebrate with my friends;

The older son's submissive attitude kept him from having deep, enduring relationships with other people. Therefore he could not initiate a party himself. He felt that if he ever deserved one that his father would give it to him.

Because the older son was feeling sorry for himself, he made spiteful comments and cutting, sarcastic remarks toward his father. He displayed his resentment toward his father for not honoring him with a party so that he could be merry with his friends.

The older son felt mistreated in some way, implying that his father did not care for him as much as he did his younger brother. He did not feel loved, and he wanted to be rewarded for doing what was right. Problem kids get the attention, however, and the older brother was jealous of his younger brother.

The older son essentially blamed his father for his not partying with his friends and did not take responsibility for the unconnected relationship with his friends. The older son lacked close friendships.

The older son was not facing the truth about his inadequacy by blaming his father. He portrayed himself as being perfect and overlooked his own faults. He considered himself moral and implied that his younger brother was very immoral. The older son implied that he had good judgment and his younger brother lacked judgment. In reality, he probably had immoral urges; he just never acted on them. The older son was comparing himself to the "old" younger brother and not his "new" younger brother, who was a changed man.

The older son never spoke up before, but now he exploded with resentment.

- Why was he now willing to confront?
- Why was he now willing to risk the consequences of speaking his mind?
- Did he feel his argument would win over his father, or was he just venting his frustration?

30 but when this son of yours came, who has devoured your wealth with prostitutes, you killed the fattened calf for him.'

A person does not just suddenly start thinking and expressing himself in this way. For years the older son had thought these thoughts but never expressed them. This explosion occurred because pressure had been building and accumulating for years.

The older son was really putting down his father and his younger brother here. He was saying things about his younger brother that he knew were not true. But he had thought this about his brother all the time his brother was gone.

It sounds as if the brothers had talked about the far country and the younger brother had told his other brother about what was in the far country and what was attracting him to go to the far country. Was the older brother jealous that his brother had the guts to do something he was not capable of? The older son was projecting his own mental attitude and desire for sexual sin onto his younger brother by accusing him of devouring the money with prostitutes. He was accusing his brother of doing what he wished he could do. He had lusted in his mind.

The older brother was comparing his behavior with that of his younger brother. The older son portrayed himself as righteous and his younger brother as immoral. The older son said it was unfair that his father would kill the calf for his brother but never for him.

Again this older, submissive brother did not have a good relationship with his younger brother. The older brother did not quickly run to his younger brother and tell him that he was glad he was back safe and sound. Instead, he ridiculed him to his father and also called him his father's son, not his brother.

The submissive, older son exaggerated the actions of his younger brother. The older son was aggressive and not assertive.

The father paid the price of being assertive when the younger son returned home. By having a joyful, festive celebration for his younger son, the father brought on a painful encounter with his older son. Yet the father was honest and caring during the confrontation with his older son.

There is always a price for being assertive. Being assertive does not mean that everyone is going to be happy with the life of the assertive person. There are still going to be disruptions and conflict between people. However, being assertive is the right approach and has the best long-term positive results. Assertive people have more influence and are more successful in their relationships at home and at work.

The older son was saying here that he preferred the reward-and-punishment method of dealing with people's behavior. If they are good, then reward them; if they do something bad, punish them. The older son was saying he preferred the system of law rather than a system of grace and mercy.

By analogy, the older son was attempting to gain salvation by his works. He was attempting to obey the law, what the father commanded, and receive salvation as a result. Every person who tries to work his way into heaven by his good deeds, keeping the law, being a good person, or being religious puts up a barrier between himself and God. Good works always fall short of the glory of God.

31 "And he said to him, 'Son, you have always been with me, and all that is mine is yours.

The father did not say, "You should not feel that way." He allowed his older son to say what he was feeling and did not make him feel guilty or ashamed afterward. The father allowed his son to vent his feelings.

The father did not "moralize" the issue. He did not say he was hurt by the sarcastic remarks made by his older son. The father did not act surprised at the anger, even though it was out of character for the older son. The father knew all along that there was resentment in his son's heart; it was just not expressed. The father was not taken by surprise by the outburst of his oldest son.

The father responded to his oldest son in a way his son understood. He did not become emotional about the issue. The father said his son was always with him. His son would always be known as "his son" and not as a whole person himself. The older son's submissiveness made him into a slave of his father and not a son. He was totally dependent on his father for everything, when he should have had some independence. All the father could say about their relationship was that his son was ever with him. That is sad.

The father had to have felt some kind of disgust with this older son. I am sure he felt pity for him and his unfulfilled life. The father was irritated at his son's lack of motivation to have his own mind and to pursue his own desires. The father must have felt guilty about his son doing exactly as he asked all the time. The father must have felt like he was controlling his older son.

The father confirmed to him that everything the family possessed was still his. The father told him that all the family resources were his, indicating that he could spend the money if he chose to do so.

Why did the older son not like himself enough to do nice things for himself? He did nice things for others, but why did he feel he did not deserve it for himself?

The father wanted real peace with his son. He did not want a son who wanted "peace at any cost" and therefore is submissive and compliant and not real.

The father affirmed the older son—though not his behavior—by assuring him that he was still with him and that every thing still belonged to him. The father communicated to his son that it was OK to communicate his feelings and thoughts and that he would not be punished for being assertive.

The analogy here is that the older son was good, but being a good person does not get a person into heaven. Everyone who attempts to gain the approbation of God by good works falls short of the glory of God. The good person often does get rewarded in his life with earthly rewards of the world's goods, such as money, recognitions, admiration, happiness, friends, and respect, but merely being "good" does not bring one into God's favor.

The analogy of the ring, coat, and shoes is that one who believes becomes a child of God. The good person does not receive these things from the Father.

The analogy of the party is that the new believer receives eternal life with God and fellow believers. The good person does not have a party and therefore does not receive eternal life with God.

32 It was meet that we should make merry, and be glad: for this thy brother was dead, and is alive again; and was lost, and is found.

The father was saying that his younger son's return represented a personal, life-changing decision. The father was not rewarding bad behavior; rather, he was celebrating the change of heart and change of attitude by the younger son.

When one makes the decision that affects his eternal future, it should be celebrated as it is celebrating the birthday of being born again. Since the older son had not had such a celebration, this indicates the older son was still dead and lost.

Since the father was assertive and responded properly to his older son, the older son had to be responsible for his own actions. He would not be able to blame his father's making him angry as the reason for not attending the celebration. The father did not defend the younger son. He stated that his younger son had been dead and lost. But he also said that the younger was now alive and found.

The father was trying to teach his son a new way of relating. The father's nonjudgmental attitude and noncondemning nature was demonstrated to the older son over and over again.

Being assertive is being authentic. It is being vulnerable and real. It creates an atmosphere that makes joy and intimacy possible. Being assertive, being authentic, being vulnerable, and showing forgiveness and unconditional love leads to joy, peace, and love.

The father's goal from the beginning was to help both of his sons learn new and effective ways of living and relating. He demonstrated the ability to treat each person uniquely according to his needs. He wanted to both break their dysfunctional habits of relating and develop new, more fulfilling ways of living and relating.

The father acknowledged the feelings of the older son. After this exchange, the older son would still feel OK about himself. His personhood or character was not attacked. The older son was not put into a defensive position. He was treated as an adult and not a child. By being treated this way, the older son was able to change his mind and come to the celebration with his dignity and not feel cut down or belittled. The father was able to deal constructively with the situation.

The father's highest purpose was for his son to be alive and found. Alive means to be born again and to be spiritually alive (God's part of salvation). Found means to come to one's senses and desire a relationship with God (Man's part of Salvation). Since the father spoke twice in this parable about being "found" and "alive," this is a most important statement in the parable.

The parable does not indicate if the older son returned with his father to the celebration. The focus remains not on the older son but on the younger son being alive and found.

If this parable had been about conflict resolution, it would have indicated the outcome of this stressful encounter. However, the way the father handled this conflict, his relationship with his older son was deepened and enriched. They no longer had a superficial relationship. The older son must have felt empowered because he was not put down or dominated by his father in this discussion. The discussion left the older son feeling validated in his feelings. The older son learned that it was OK to communicate his feelings, good or bad, to his father and that his father would not think any less of him for doing it. This had to have felt good to the older son to feel and sense the respect that his father had for him. The older son also had to respect his father for being able to express his reasons for what he did without hurting his own feelings. The older son had to admire his father for making him feel important enough that his father would leave the celebration to come and attend to his hurt feelings. The older son had to be in awe of how skillfully his father handled the whole situation. But we are not told of the response of the older son. The older son had all the information he needed and all the examples of grace he needed in order to come to himself and make the best choice. But the decision and choice was his. He was totally responsible for his choice, and he could not say that no one had given him the gospel.

Back at the celebration, the younger son had to admire his father for making him feel important and worthy of being called his son by having the celebration and giving him the ring, the coat, and the shoes. The younger son had to be in awe of how skillfully his father handled the whole situation.

Moral of the Story

The younger son, through determination, asserted his desire for his personal space. He was self-confident, assured, satisfied, well adjusted, full, responsible, self-controlled, powerful, and aware. He succumbed to the temptation of his fleshly lust. He asserted his independence and sought to satisfy the lust he was feeling. He ignored everything he was taught. He left the safety of home and headed to a distant city. He lost his possessions and strong personal space because of bad choices. The younger son lived a life of adventure. He lost his money through very bad choices, but he found himself in the process. The maturity gained and wisdom learned from this failure would be priceless. It would ultimately launch him into nourishing relationships, ennobling work, creative leisure, and causes worthy of his devotion. He would become an impacting individual, and he would always be others-conscious.

The older son was not determined. He was not self-confident, not assured, satisfied, well adjusted, responsible, self-controlled, powerful and aware. He lost his space (respect of his father) because of personal weakness. The older son lived a bleak, narrow, and dismal existence. He would always be a discontent worker, have unfulfilling relationships, and guarded leisure. He would not be involved in causes driven by passion. He would always be a self-conscious, selfish little clod of ailments and grievances, complaining that his father was not devoting himself to making him happy.

We all have imperfections, immaturities, and impediments in areas of our personalities. Most of us learn life's lessons through experience, trial and error. Unfortunately, a few these life lessons are deadly and a person's life is ended unnecessarily and prematurely. Every effort is needed to protect the naive from immature decisions. Thus, parents should teach their children about calculated risks while allowing their children to take responsibility for their own behavior.

Mark 7:21-23 explains the source of defilement: **"For from within, out of the heart of men, proceed the evil thoughts and fornications, thefts, murders, adulteries, . . . sensuality, envy, slander, pride, and foolishness. All these evil things proceed from within and defile the man."**

John 3:3, 17, and 36 reveal the solution for defiled man: **"Jesus answered and said to him, 'Truly, truly, I say to you, unless one is born again, he cannot see the kingdom of God. . . . For God did not send the Son into the world to judge the world; but that the world should be saved through Him. . . . He who believes in the Son has eternal life."**

We are not defined by our past. We can have failures in our past, but they do not make us a failure. We can even "find ourselves" as a result of bad decisions. We can learn from our mistakes. In overcoming our mistakes, we can develop empathy for others who have failures in their past. We are not defined by our past. In fact, the past can actually be a stepping-stone into a new, successful future when it leads us to a relationship with God.

The mistakes we make and the suffering that results can lead us into the spiritual dimension. When we see that our choices have hurt others, as well as ourselves, and have been sins against God, we see ourselves as we truly are. As we realize that we are sinners who are selfish and self-centered and in need of a savior, we become receptive to acknowledging the gospel and acting on it. When we "find ourselves" and believe the good news of Jesus Christ, we are born again and "alive." God's desire is to have a relationship with us, to change us, and to give us a future here on earth and an eternal one in heaven with Him.

The parable of the prodigal son does not tell us the fate of the older brother. The older brother was approached by his father (God) and invited to change his life, change his mind about his current life choices. John 3:36 reveals the outcome depending on his choice: "He who believes in the Son has eternal life; but he who does not obey the Son shall not see life, but the wrath of God abides on him."

John 3:20-21 says, **"For everyone who does evil hates the light, and does not come to the light, lest his deeds should be exposed. But he who practices the truth comes to the light, that his deeds may be manifested as having been wrought in God."** The younger son "found himself." He came to the light and acknowledged his sin and was saved. The older son was facing the choice of coming to the light or not. Everyone has that choice. Your eternal future depends on your choice. Do you want an eternal relationship with God and His blessings like the younger son? Or do you want the wrath of God? It is your choice. I exhort you to choose life!

Perhaps you find yourself today with a prodigal child. Your son or daughter has left home and is living an unhealthy, destructive, and unspiritual lifestyle. You are in great pain. You've probably cried yourself to sleep every night for months and maybe even years. But there is hope. Do not give up. Keep praying for your child. It is out of your control. You are out of options humanly speaking. But God is faithful. Do not give up your faith in God and His ability to answer your prayers.

I can't patronize you and guarantee 100 percent that your child will return home safe. Sometimes the prodigal lifestyle does end with disastrous consequences. I have to be realistic about the world system and the evil present in it.

On the other hand, I know of many instances when God delivered prodigals from their poor choices and brought them to their senses, and they returned home. So put your hope in God and His provision. Claim the promise in Proverbs 22:6, "**Train up a child in the way he should go, even when he is old he will not depart from it**." Above all, pray.

Here are some Scriptures you may find helpful.

- Matthew 11:28: "**Come to Me, all who are weary and heavy-laden, and I will give you rest**."
- Matthew 7:7 "**Ask, and it shall be given to you; seek, and you shall find; knock, and it shall be opened to you**."
- Matthew 9:29: "**Be it done to you according to your faith**."
- Matthew 18:14: "**Thus it is not the will of your Father who is in heaven that one of these little ones perish**."
- Matthew 21:22: "**And everything you ask in prayer, believing, you shall receive**."
- Mark 10:27: "**Looking upon them, Jesus said, 'With men it is impossible, but not with God; for all things are possible with God.'**"
- Mark 11:22: "**And Jesus answered saying to them, 'Have faith in God.'**"
- Mark 11:24: "**Therefore I say to you, 'All things for which you pray and ask, believe that you have received them, and they shall be granted you.'**"
- Philippians 4:6-7: "**Be anxious for nothing, but in everything by prayer and supplication with thanksgiving let your requests be made known to God, and the peace of God which surpasses all comprehension, shall guard your hearts and your minds in Christ Jesus**."
- Hebrews 4:16: "**Let us therefore draw near with confidence to the throne of grace, that we may receive mercy and may find grace to help in time of need**."

- 2 Peter 3:9: **"The Lord is not slow about His promise, as some count slowness, but is patient toward you, not wishing for any to perish but for all to come to repentance."**
- 1 John 4:18: **"There is no fear in love; but perfect love casts out fear."**
- Psalm 147:11: **"The Lord favors those who fear Him, those who wait for His lovingkindness."**
- Matthew 19:26: **"And looking upon them Jesus said to them, 'With men this is impossible, but with God all things are possible.'"**
- James 5:16: **"The effective prayer of a righteous man can accomplish much."**

God answers prayer. So keep praying. Give your child over to God in faith. Trust Him, keep praying, and keep looking in faith for your child's return. Keep reading these Scriptures, and they will give you hope and increase your faith. All things are possible with God. Keep this in the forefront of your mind as you pray.

CHAPTER 4

Parable of the Prodigal Son as Two Spiritually Immature Believers

In the previous chapter we looked at the two sons in Jesus' parable as two unbelievers. The younger one, though rebellious, eventually repented and returned to his father. The other remained with his father but also remained unrepentant. However, the parable also presents important truths related to spiritual maturity when interpreted as portraying two believing sons who are at different stages of spiritual growth. The two young believers had their own weaknesses and sinned in different ways from each other. The consequences of sin always vary by the type of sin, especially when it violates a law of society. But all sin is dealt with the same way in the spiritual sense by receiving God's forgiveness.

Becoming a mature person spiritually is a long process. When a person is saved, he or she begins the spiritual journey with a lot of bad habits developed over the previous years of life. Everyone has both strengths and weaknesses of personality. Everyone has suffered rejection, abandonment, abuse, neglect, a broken heart, betrayal, or some other injustice and carries baggage from those hurts and difficult relationships. All start the spiritual journey at the same point, all in need of having their mind reprogrammed for viewing life from God's viewpoint and conforming their life, attitudes, and behaviors so that they are consistent with God's principles.

This means every person has a lot to learn and a lot of hard work of change in order to become a spiritually mature person. In this lifetime no one can reach the end of the destination and become perfect. The goal is to keep pressing on toward the finish line, despite any and all obstacles in the way during the journey. Since spiritual maturity is a journey of faith, it consists of a lot of unknowns.

Spiritual maturity is about developing one's faith. Faith comes by hearing and believing the Word of God, and faith is always tested to see if it is really faith. As faith is confirmed, a person's confidence in God and love for God increases. One of the first things a believer needs to know is how to handle sin. A person does not stop sinning once he is saved. Just as sin was an issue as a part of salvation, sin is still an issue after salvation. God has provided a way for dealing with sin. At salvation a person repents, acknowledges he is a sinner, and believes that Jesus died in his place and paid the penalty for his sins. When a person does this, all his sins up to that moment in time are forgiven. After salvation, to receive forgiveness for sins committed a person needs to confess those sins to God, and He forgives those sins on the basis of Jesus' having paid the penalty for those sins by His death on the cross.

This sounds like a simple process to follow, and for some people it is. For others, something interferes with the implementing of this procedure. Some people don't know the process because no one has informed them of the proper way of dealing with sin. Other people hold to a view that this process is not necessary. Others are too busy with the affairs of this world to be interested in maintaining their spiritual growth. Some believe they are so religious that they don't need to confess their sins to God. Others believe they are basically good people and don't have anything to confess. Some people are so wrought with guilt and shame they feel unworthy to come to God. They believe God is punishing them for their sin and this is their only option. Some people believe they have to feel remorse for their sin and promise to never commit that sin again before God will forgive them.

This parable sets forth the biblical way of receiving forgiveness and restoring fellowship with God after committing sin. This is good news for all the people listed above, including myself. In this chapter, the parable of the prodigal son is interpreted as speaking of two immature believers dealing with their sin. We will look at what the parable says to us in light of this understanding.

Verse-by-Verse Analysis

Luke 15:11 And He said, "A man had two sons.

By analogy, the man is a father who is a mature Christian believer who has two sons. The two sons are children of God and have already believed in the Lord Jesus Christ. The father also represents God.

12 "The younger of them said to his father, 'Father, give me the share of the estate that falls to me.' So he divided his wealth between them.

The younger son asked for his inheritance, which was legally his. This was not a sin in itself, and his father divided his estate and gave both sons their inheritance. The custom was for the older son to be given two-thirds of the family assets and the younger son one-third of the family assets. By analogy, when the younger son said "give me," he was taking back control of his life from God. When God is in control, a person has access to the mind of God and access to God's plan for his life. When God is in control, the person is still making his own decisions, but he follows the leading of God in making his choices.

The younger son was prideful. He had been comparing himself to his older brother. He was wiser, stronger, more talented, more determined, more gifted, and more of a leader than his older brother. Because of this his heart was lifted up, and he became proud and arrogant. In his rebelliousness he became independent and self-centered. This pride led him to take his eyes off God and start looking at the world and what it had to offer. The world was appealing to him. He felt he could make it on his own in the world. Because he was constantly thinking about the temptations of his flesh, he decided to leave home and be on his own to enjoy what he saw out in the world.

13 "And not many days later, the younger son gathered everything together and went on a journey into a distant country, and there he squandered his estate with loose living.

The younger son went into the world and misused the capital his father had given to him. This activity had disastrous results for him, as he wasted all his wealth and became broke.

By analogy, the meaning of the younger son going on a journey into a distant country is that the younger son is leaving the fellowship of God. A person is spiritual when God is in control of his life. A person becomes carnal when he sins, and as a result he takes back control of his own life and loses fellowship with God. The relationship with God is not severed when a person sins; the person is still a child of God.

However, when a person takes back control of his life from God, the person returns to being controlled by the lusts of his flesh, which means being carnal. When a person takes control of his life away from God, that person is displeasing God. Pride is the sin that most displeases God. The deeds of the flesh follow: immorality, impurity, sensuality, enmity, strife, jealousy, outbursts of anger, disputes, drunkenness, and carousing; all these describe the younger brother's activities. He was definitely behaving in a carnal manner.

When a believer walks by the Spirit, he does not carry out the desires of the flesh. The younger son was not walking under the control of the Holy Spirit during this time.

14 "Now when he had spent everything, a severe famine occurred in that country, and he began to be impoverished.

The younger son spent everything he had; and when the famine came, he began an existence of poverty.

The carnal person suffers the normal consequences that accompany being in control of his life.

God allows the natural consequences of sin to occur in the carnal person's life. God uses these natural consequences of the carnal believer's choice to sin to discipline that believer. God allows the carnal believer to suffer and to deal with the circumstances that he has gotten himself into. God does not punish; rather, God disciplines His child in love like any good father does.

15 "So he went and hired himself out to one of the citizens of that country, and he sent him into his fields to feed swine.

The younger son became desperate and took a job that was repulsive to him, as a Jew. By analogy, a person dealing with the natural consequences of his sin often experiences circumstances that are very repulsive to him. As someone has said, sin will take you farther, keep you longer, and cost you more than you ever intended.

16 "And he would have gladly filled his stomach with the pods that the swine were eating, and no one was giving anything to him.

He was so hungry he longed to eat the food he was feeding to the pigs. By analogy, after one sins so often, because of guilt, the person isolates himself from other people. Besides losing fellowship with God, the carnal person loses fellowship with fellow believers, who are normally a support system.

17 "But when he came to his senses, he said, 'How many of my father's hired men have more than enough bread, but I am dying here with hunger!

The younger son came to his senses and decided to start looking for other options. By analogy, "when he came to his senses" means that the person ultimately decides to stop trying to solve his problems on his own and to call out to God for His help. He is repentant. The carnal believer is so frustrated from his futile attempts to rescue himself that he decides to look at life again from a biblical perspective. This means the carnal believer stops using any defense mechanism he is using and acknowledges and confesses his sin.

18 'I will get up and go to my father, and will say to him, "Father, I have sinned against heaven, and in your sight;

In repentance, the younger son decides to return home to his father and admit his actions were sinful toward God and improper toward his father.

By analogy, the carnal believer plans to return to fellowship with God by confessing his sins. The carnal believer is doing exactly what the Bible instructs him to do to address his sin. Going to the Father means to say a prayer to God agreeing with Him.

19 I am no longer worthy to be called your son; make me as one of your hired men."

The younger son determined to declare that he was not worthy to be called a son of his father and to ask to be hired as a servant. By analogy, the carnal believer now makes an emotional response, trying to impress God with his remorsefulness. This self-reproach is not necessary and does not get him back into fellowship with God. This is the believer telling God how he feels God ought to treat him because of his recent sins. This is ridiculous. Our relationship with God is secured at salvation because nothing can separate us from the love of God. Our relationship with God depends on God, and not on us, and the Bible says He is holding on to us. Salvation is a gift, and since we did nothing to receive this gift, there is nothing we can do to lose this gift.

20 "So he got up and came to his father. But while he was still a long way off, his father saw him and felt compassion for him, and ran and embraced him and kissed him.

By analogy, God is compassionate and anxious to have the repentant believer back in fellowship with Him. When the carnal believer decides in his heart to confess his sin, God is always ready to lovingly welcome him back into His fellowship.

21 "And the son said to him, 'Father, I have sinned against heaven and in your sight; I am no longer worthy to be called your son.'

By analogy, the carnal believer prays and acknowledges his sin to God. But when he starts this junk about not being worthy, God immediately interrupts him. Remorse, feeling sorry for committing a sin, is not part of the confession process. This parable emphasizes the fact that our value and worth is not diminished by our sin.

It is OK to acknowledge the fact that God is holy and we are not holy. It is because we are not holy that we need a savior. And that Savior is Jesus Christ.

22 "But the father said to his slaves, 'Quickly bring out the best robe and put it on him, and put a ring on his hand and sandals on his feet;
23 and bring the fattened calf, kill it, and let us eat and celebrate;

By analogy, as soon as a carnal believer confesses his sins, God restores the believer to full fellowship with Himself. Some of the benefits of being in fellowship with God are:

- clothed in righteousness, washed clean from the sin
- full son status and authority (as indicated by the ring)
- God's strength and direction in the execution of his spiritual gifts
- the full feasting on and understanding of the Word of God
- direction from the Holy Spirit
- access to the mind of Christ
- access to the Comforter, the Holy Spirit

The time of celebration is the time to praise God publicly for his kindness and mercy in rescuing the believer.

24 for this son of mine was dead and has come to life again; he was lost and has been found.' And they began to celebrate.

When the believer is carnal and in control of his own fleshly life, he is out of fellowship with God. Being out of fellowship, according to this verse, is like death, or being away from God. "Lost" also means being away from the family of God and missing out on the blessing that comes from being involved with the family of God. Each family member is needed for the family to function properly. Each family member is fulfilled in serving the other family members through prayer, fellowship, and the exercise of spiritual gifts.

When a believer comes back into fellowship with God, it is a time to celebrate with fellow believers.

**25 "Now his older son was in the field, and when he came and approached the house, he heard music and dancing.
26 "And he summoned one of the servants and began inquiring what these things could be.
27 "And he said to him, 'Your brother has come, and your father has killed the fattened calf because he has received him back safe and sound.'
28 "But he became angry and was not willing to go in; and his father came out and began pleading with him.**

The other believer (the older son) should have been glad to welcome the repentant believer back into the family. Instead, he became jealous and angry. As a result, this believer became a carnal believer himself.

What is indicated here is that there are different kinds of sin. Each person has strengths and weaknesses in his personality. It is easy for a person with strength in one area to judge and condemn another believer who is weak in that area and sins in that area. It is hard for that person to see his own sin. This person is being self-righteous when he judges other people's sins and is blind to his own sin.

God will convict this carnal believer of his sinful mental attitude, hoping that erring believer will immediately confess his sin and return to fellowship with Him.

God desires this believer to treat his repentant brother with the same grace as God Himself treated that repentant person.

God deals with this second carnal believer just as he did the first carnal believer described above. Carnality is carnality to God, no matter the type of sin. To God, sin is sin.

29 "But he answered and said to his father, 'Look! For so many years I have been serving you and I have never neglected a command of yours; and yet you have never given me a young goat, so that I might celebrate with my friends;

The older son was disrespectful to his father. He had been serving his father with the wrong motivation. He had been a "good" son, but his obedience was for selfish gain or out of fear. The older son was not doing it out of love for his father.

By analogy, the carnal believer is prideful in his past service to God; he is arrogant, self-exalting and haughty in his response to God. The carnal believer trusts in his own talents, his education, and his own achievements. And he is very obviously ungrateful for the blessings he has received in the past from God. His sin is in his lust for recognition. He does "good deeds" for recognition, personal reward, public recognition, and to be seen and then praised by man. The Bible says this carnal believer is lying to the Holy Spirit. "Good works" are burned as wood, hay, and stubble by God in the Day of Judgment.

30 but when this son of yours came, who has devoured your wealth with prostitutes, you killed the fattened calf for him.'

When the believer becomes carnal and leaves fellowship with God and begins sinning, one sin leads to another sin. At first the older brother was jealous; then he became angry; then he began to judge his brother; then he maligned his brother. And finally he maligned God. This carnal believer was guilty of being legalistic and self-righteous. He was disrespectful of the way God allows other repentant believers back into His fellowship by just confessing their sins.

31 "And he said to him, 'Son, you have always been with me, and all that is mine is yours.
32 It was meet that we should make merry, and be glad: for this thy brother was dead, and is alive again; and was lost, and is found.

By analogy, when the believer chooses to follow his fleshly desires and becomes carnal, he is "temporarily dead" and lost. To begin to live again in the fellowship of God and be "found," all the carnal believer has to do is confess his sins. At that instant, God is prepared and waiting to welcome the carnal believer back into His fellowship.

From the time a person is born until he becomes a believer, he is in control of his life and under the power of the desires of the old sin nature. This leads to sins of the flesh, which include immorality, impurity, sensuality, idolatry, strife, jealousy, anger, envy, drunkenness, and things like these. A person living in this manner is living a carnal life.

When a person experiences salvation, he is indwelt by the Holy Spirit and receives the filling of the Holy Spirit. The new believer turns over control of his life to the Holy Spirit. When the Holy Spirit is in control of a believer's life, the believer is living a spiritual life. All believers experience temptation, and when they do, they have to decide whether to give in to the temptation and sin or to resist the temptation. The believer has the power to resist and a means of escape from the temptation and not sin. Yet all believers at times succumb to temptation and sin. Pride is the sin that many believers succumb to. God blesses a believer, and sometimes the believer begins to think that the success and blessing is because of his or her own efforts and not a blessing from God.

God has provided the means for the believer to overcome the power of sin. When the believer sins and takes back control of his life from the Holy Spirit, he loses the filling of the Holy Spirit; and this "grieves" the Holy Spirit. When a believer takes control of his own life, the believer returns to living the carnal life.

The means God provides for the believer to become spiritual again is to confess his sin. When the believer does this, the Holy Spirit fills the believer and the Holy Spirit takes control of the believer. Now the believer is living the spiritual life again. When a believer walks by the Spirit, he does not carry out the desires of the flesh.

For new believers with a history and a pattern of living a carnal, sinful life, it is a struggle to consistently live the spiritual life. The old sin nature of the new believer desires to be in control. The Holy Spirit also desires to be in control. The result is a great struggle for dominance in the life of the believer. Unfortunately, most new believers are not given the necessary instructions for confessing their sins and returning control of their life to the Holy Spirit after they sin. God's people suffer for lack of knowledge. One of the reasons this book was written is to educate believers in the principles of God's Word that lead to a successful spiritual life.

Summary

In 1 John 2:15-16 a stern warning is given to believers. "**Do not love the world, nor the things in the world. If any one loves the world, the love of the Father is not in him. For all that is in the world, the lust of the flesh, and the lust of the eyes and the boastful pride of life, is not from the Father, but is from the world.**" Proverbs 16:18 warns that "**prides goes before destruction, and a haughty spirit before stumbling.**"

Romans 13:12-14 really addresses the life that the younger son lived: "**The night is almost gone, and the day is at hand. Let us therefore lay aside the deeds of darkness and put on the armor of light. Let us behave properly as in the day, not in carousing and drunkenness, not in sexual promiscuity and sensuality, not in strife and jealousy. But put on the Lord Jesus Christ, and make no provision for the flesh in regard to its lusts.**"

First Corinthians gives this warning to the carnal: "And I brethren could not speak to you as to spiritual men, but as to men of flesh, as to babes in Christ, . . . for you are still fleshly. For since there is jealousy and strife among you, are you not fleshly, and are you not walking like mere men? . . . each man's work will become evident; for the day will show it, because it is to be revealed with fire; and the fire itself will test the quality of each man's work. If any man' work which he has built upon it remains, he shall receive a reward. If any man's work is burned up, he shall suffer loss; but he himself shall be saved, yet so as through fire. Do you not know that you are a temple of God, and that he Spirit of God dwells in you?" (3:1, 3, 13-16).

The world is full of temptation. It is very easy to live a carnal life and indulge in the lusts of the flesh. This life is short, and eternity is right around the corner. Everyone is accountable for his or her attitudes, actions, and behaviors. Everyone needs to watch out for pride and lust. This is the time to think about the eternal rather than the temporal. The works of every believer will be tested. The works of the carnal believer will be burned up. The works of the Spirit-led believer will remain, and he will receive a reward in eternity. Yes, the carnal believer is saved, but he will suffer the loss of rewards.

If you are living the carnal life, I exhort you to return to God and confess your pride and sins. He will forgive you. Live the Christian life; your works will survive the fire and you can have great rewards. Don't have regrets! Choose life!

Perhaps you are living your life separated from your family and friends. It does not matter today what got you to this point. The important thing is that you are examining your life and considering your current options. Maybe you have some good options. But maybe you are at the end of your rope and you feel helpless, hopeless, and defeated. There is one path you may or not have thought about. Consider turning to God.

Let's look at the story of Jonah. He did not obey God, and he found himself in a mess. He would have drowned if the fish had not swallowed him. From his mess (Jon. 2:1-9) he prayed, and God heard his prayer. Jonah was near death, and he remembered the Lord. In his prayer, Jonah vowed to speak about the faithfulness of God with a voice of thanksgiving, and he promised to keep his vows. He then acknowledged that salvation is from the Lord. After he prayed, God commanded the fish, and it vomited Jonah up on dry land. Then God commanded Jonah to go to Nineveh and to preach against it. He did, and the people of Nineveh believed in God. The people of Nineveh prayed earnestly that they might turn from their wicked way and from the violence of their hands. God saw their deeds, and God relented about destroying the city. This made Jonah angry. He wanted his nation's enemies in Nineveh to be punished, yet he knew God is a gracious and compassionate God, slow to anger and abundant in lovingkindness, and one who relents concerning calamity.

Maybe you would have died if God had not saved your life. Maybe this book is like the preaching of Jonah, calling you to repent. If you do, God will treat you just as he did the citizens of Nineveh. He will save you and relent from all the calamity that you may deserve. God is gracious and compassionate. Turn to Him and pray. He will save you. Maybe some of your enemies want you to be punished. But God is abundant in lovingkindness and is one who relents. Consider taking advantage of His mercy today. Maybe your time is running out. Maybe God is calling out to you today and wants you to believe in Him and turn to Him. Decide right now to reconcile with God, and then do it. Then return home and be reconciled to your family and friends. You will be a different person when you return home. Take the first step right now; decide to cry out to God for help. He will hear you, and He will save you. This is your best option. Decide right now, and act.

CHAPTER 5

Parable of the Prodigal Son as Pharisees and Scribes

When Jesus told the parable of the prodigal son, we know that He was speaking to publicans (tax collectors) and sinners (prostitutes) who were in this gathering (Luke 15:1). The publicans and sinners were in the lowest social order in Jewish society. The Pharisees (religious leaders) and scribes (lawyers) came to the gathering to criticize Jesus for eating with the publicans and sinners. A scribe, Pharisee, or any self-respecting Jew would not be seen with publicans and sinners, let alone dine with them. The context thus supports an interpretation of the parable that relates it to the scribes and Pharisees.

Who Were the Scribes?

Scribes were biblical scholars respected for their comprehensive knowledge of the Old Testament law, which they taught and defended. Most scribes belonged to the party of the Pharisees, and in the New Testament the scribes are frequently mentioned together with the Pharisees.

Who Were the Pharisees?

The Pharisees were a religious and political party in Jesus' day. The word Pharisee comes from pharisaios (far-is-ah'-yos), meaning a separatist (i.e., exclusively religious). The Pharisees were the religious leaders in their community.

The Pharisees were especially known for insisting that the law of God be observed as the scribes interpreted it. They also were known for their special commitment to keeping the laws of tithing and scrupulously paying the tithes due to the priest, the Levite, and the poor. They were known for their strict observance of Levitical ritual purity and for a conscientious regard for vows and for other people's property. The Pharisees were concerned about strictly interpreting and keeping the law on all matters, including the Sabbath, divorce, oaths, the wearing of phylacteries and fringes, and other matters.

Since Pharisees found that other Jews were not as careful as they were about keeping the laws of tithing and ritual purity, they felt it was necessary to place limits on their contacts with other Jews, as well as with Gentiles. They were so legalistic that they would not eat in the home of a non-Pharisee, since they could not be sure that the food had been properly tithed or kept ritually pure.

Summary of Jesus' Criticism of the Scribes and Pharisees

Jesus criticized the scribes and Pharisees for:

- their burdensome rules and regulations, which they portrayed as God's law and requirements for entering God's kingdom. He also charged them with lacking true piety, which explains why they would set aside the commandments of God for their own rules and regulations.
- professing to be the spiritual guides, shepherds, or leaders of their time and yet leading people astray
- being primarily interested in position, power, and authority and not concerned about their relationship with God

- observing the smallest matters of the law while ignoring the more important ones
- stealing from the widows and the poor and accepting the contributions of widows for religious services rendered
- making a great spectacle of themselves by offering long prayers in public
- following the letter of the law while ignoring the intent of the law
- failing to recognize their own spiritual blindness
- making sure that they were outwardly righteous and presentable while inwardly they were spiritually dead (thus making the point of the relative importance of the state of the heart over obedience to individual commandments)

Jesus called the scribes and Pharisees "hypocrites," "vipers," "blind guides which strain out the gnat and swallow the camel," and "whitewashed tombs which outwardly appear beautiful, but inwardly are full of dead men's bones." Jesus compared the scribes and Pharisees to whitewashed tombs because their behavior conformed to the law but their hearts nonetheless were corrupt.

Meaning of the Parable of the Prodigal Son

The Father

In this interpretation of the parable, the father represents God, the common Father of all mankind. From the parable, we see that God is compassionate and forgiving toward sinners when they turn toward Him. We see that God attempts to persuade the sinner who is self-righteous or "moral" to turn to Him also.

The Younger Son

The younger son represents the sinners and publicans. These publicans and sinners knew their condition. They knew that they practiced immorality, sensuality, strife, jealousy, anger, envy, disputes, dissensions, drunkenness, and carousing. They knew they were living to fulfill their own lusts and to serve themselves. Yet, when they confessed their sinfulness and turned to God, He accepted them and gave them a place of prominence in His family.

The Older Son

The older son represents the scribes and Pharisees. The parable describes these religious leaders as angry and self-righteous. They were do-gooders, obeying the letter of the law, living outwardly moral lives, and doing good for selfish reasons and for personal gain. These religious leaders were blind to their own spiritual condition.

On the surface, they appeared to be in God's kingdom. But outward appearance does not reveal the actual state of a person's heart. The Pharisees and scribes were hypocrites. They were self-righteous, but self-righteousness is not righteousness in God's eyes.

The older son also portrays religious people in general. Most religious people are good, moral people, read the Bible or the spiritual book of their religion, appear to obey the rules of their religion, serve the needs of others, and give generously of their time and resources. Religious people officiate at religious ceremonies and perform the religious rituals of their church, synagogue, or mosque. They preach or give sermons on religious matters, interpret scriptures, and speak for God in their religious community. Still, these people are sinners and in need of personal salvation from God.

The older son also portrays good and moral people. Good and moral people are deceived by their own goodness and kindness toward other people. They believe that by all these good works they have earned their way into heaven. Many good people have given large sums of money to build hospitals. Others have raised funds and gone to nations to feed millions of starving children. Others have built orphanages, homes for addicts, and homes for the abused or runaway teens. Others have gone on TV and used their name or celebrity to raise millions of dollars for the charities of choice. The older son in Jesus' parable, however, reminds us that even the "best" of people are lost sinners.

PART THREE

THEOLOGY

CHAPTER 6

What Is Salvation?

The parable of the prodigal son illustrates important spiritual principles. It also raises significant theological issues, the most important of which is the doctrine of salvation. Every person who reaches the age of mental and moral accountability will stand before God and give an account of his life. During our lifetime each of us makes a decision either to come to God or not to come to God. And we have to come to God in the way that He prescribes, which is the gospel. The people who come to God according to the gospel have their sins forgiven, are declared righteous, and will spend eternity with God; the people who do not will, as a result of their choice, spend eternity in the lake of fire, separated from God forever.

The Gospel

For God so loved the world, that He gave His only begotten Son, that whoever believes in Him should not perish, but have eternal life (John 3:16).

For all have sinned and fall short of the glory of God (Rom. 3:23).

For the wages of sin is death, but the free gift of God is eternal life in Christ Jesus our Lord (Rom. 6:23).

For Christ also died for sins once for all, the just for the unjust, in order that He might bring us to God, having been put to death in the flesh, but made alive in the spirit (1 Pet. 3:18.).

That if you confess with your mouth Jesus as Lord, and believe in your heart that God raised Him from the dead, you will be saved; for with the heart a person believes, resulting in righteousness, and with the mouth he confesses, resulting in salvation. . . . for "Whoever will call on the name of the Lord will be saved (Rom. 10:9-10, 13).

To receive salvation and receive all its benefits, each person must do the following after hearing the gospel.

1. Repent. Repent means to change your mind and make the choice for yourself that you want to come to God according to the gospel.
2. Believe the gospel, that you are a sinner, that Jesus Christ died on the cross paying for you the penalty for your sins.
3. Acknowledge to God that you admit that you are a sinner, and that you believe that Jesus Christ died on the cross to pay the penalty for your sins, and that He rose from the dead.
4. Confess. Tell someone that you believe the gospel and now have a relationship with God.

It is that simple.

I hope that you have taken the above steps and have a relationship with God. If you did it for the first time right now, then tell someone.

Important Verses Regarding Salvation

I believe a person begins his Christian walk with God better when he hears the whole gospel, not just the four traditional steps leading to salvation. When a person hears the full gospel, that person knows ahead of time what is going to be asked of him or her as a believer by God. I believe that when a person knows the whole gospel when he or she becomes a believer, that person will continue in the journey of faith and grow into a mature spiritual believer. An uneducated believer may never grow.

Here are some important verses from the Bible I believe you might find informative in knowing about the full gospel of salvation and living the Christian life.

> He who believes in the Son has eternal life; but he who does not obey the Son shall not see life, but the wrath of God abides on him (John 3:36).

> He who has the Son has the life [eternal life]; he who does not have the Son of God does not have the life (1 John 5:12).

> For I am not ashamed of the gospel, for it is the power of God for salvation to everyone who believes, to the Jew first and also to the Greek (Rom. 1:16).

> So faith comes from hearing, and hearing by the word of Christ (Rom. 10:17).

> Now after John had been taken into custody, Jesus came into Galilee, preaching the gospel of God, and saying, "The time is fulfilled, and the kingdom of God is at hand; repent and believe in the gospel" (Mark 1:14-15).

> Then He opened their minds to understand the Scriptures, and He said to them, "Thus it is written, that the Christ would suffer and rise again from the dead the third day, and that repentance for forgiveness of sins would be proclaimed in His name to all the nations, beginning from Jerusalem (Luke 24:46-47).

> Therefore having overlooked the times of ignorance, God is now declaring to men that all people everywhere should repent, because He has fixed a day in which He will judge

the world in righteousness through a Man whom He has appointed, having furnished proof to all men by raising Him from the dead (Acts 17:30-31).

I did not shrink from declaring to you anything that was profitable, and teaching you publicly and from house to house, solemnly testifying to both Jews and Greeks of repentance toward God and faith in our Lord Jesus Christ (Acts 20:20-21).

Peter said to them, "Repent, and each of you be baptized in the name of Jesus Christ for the forgiveness of your sins; and you will receive the gift of the Holy Spirit (Luke 24:38).

For the wrath of God is revealed from heaven against all ungodliness and unrighteousness of men, who suppress the truth in unrighteousness, because that which is known about God is evident within them; for God made it evident to them. For since the creation of the world His invisible attributes, His eternal power and divine nature, have been clearly seen, being understood through what has been made, so they are without excuse (Rom. 1:18-20).

If we say that we have no sin, we are deceiving ourselves, and the truth is not in us (1 John 1:8).

But the Scripture has shut up all men under sin, that the promise by faith in Jesus Christ might be given to those who believe (Gal. 3:22).

For we must all appear before the judgment seat of Christ, that each one may be recompensed for his deeds in the body, according to what he has done, whether good or bad (2 Cor. 5:10).

This is good and acceptable in the sight of God our Savior, who desires all men to be saved and to come to the knowledge of the truth. For there is one God, and one mediator also between God and men, the man Christ Jesus, who gave Himself as a ransom for all (1 Tim. 2:3-6).

But God demonstrates His own love toward us, in that while we were yet sinners, Christ died for us (Rom. 5:8).

But the Scripture has shut up all men under sin, that the promise by faith in Jesus Christ might be given to those who believe. . . . For you are all sons of God through faith in Christ Jesus (Gal. 3:22, 26).

For by grace you have been saved through faith; and that not of yourselves, it is the gift of God; not as a result of works, that no one should boast (Eph. 2:8-9).

Therefore if any man is in Christ, he is a new creature; the old things passed away; behold, new things have come (2 Cor. 5:17).

Hence, also, He is able to save forever those who draw near to God through Him, since He always lives to make intercession for them (Heb. 7:25).

What Occurs for the Believer as a Result of Salvation

Second Corinthians 5:17 says that one who is in Christ "is a new creature; the old things passed away; behold, new things have come. At the moment of salvation God does a lot of things for the new believer.
For example:

The believer has all sins and transgressions blotted out – like he had never sinned.
The believer is the recipient of eternal life – he will spend eternity with God.

The believer is guaranteed a resurrection body forever - an incorruptible body.

The believer receives eternal security - once saved, always saved; he can't lose salvation.

The believer is reconciled - the barrier between man and God is removed.

The believer is redeemed - purchased from the slave market of sin.

The believer's condemnation is removed - eternal judgment of wrath is removed.

New Believer's Future after Salvation

There are lots of different churches and denominations, all with different beliefs. I strongly urge you to find and attend a church that faithfully follows the Bible.

The Bible is full of principles for successfully living the Christian life. One principle is that of inward transformation. Accomplishing this transformation requires the daily renewing of the mind through learning and applying the other principles in the Bible. Learning these principles requires a regular time of reading and studying the Bible.

God's Plan for Believers after Salvation

God has a plan for each believer after salvation. God's plan includes specific conduct and behavior. Upon salvation God equips each believer for His service so that each believer can contribute to the building up of the body of Christ. We can be sure that He gives us everything we need, for Romans 8:32 tells us, "He who did not spare His own Son, but delivered Him up for us all, how will He not also with Him freely give us all things?"

Principles for New Believers

1. At the moment of salvation, the new believer is given one or more spiritual gifts.

2. The believer is equipped with the spiritual gift(s) for the work of service.
3. The believer's work is to assist in the building up of the body of Christ.
4. God intends each believer to come to maturity to the measure of the stature that belongs to the fullness of Christ.
5. God intends each believer to have knowledge of the truth so that he is not deceived by every wind of doctrine or the trickery of men who are crafty in their deceitful scheming.
6. God expects each believer to grow up in all aspects to Him.

There are over 31,000 verses in the Bible, and they pertain to innumerable subjects. When all the verses about a particular subject are studied as a whole, the result is called a Biblical doctrine.

Doctrine of Repentance (before salvation)

What Is Repentance?

The Greek verb, metanoeo, translated "repent," means a complete change of mind. W. E. Vine's Expository Dictionary of New Testament Words says metanoeo literally means to perceive afterwards; hence it signifies to change one's mind or purpose, and it always involves a change for the better. The Theological Dictionary of the New Testament (Kittel) says metanoeo means, "to change one's mind," or "to convert."

Metanoeo is a transitive verb and must have a subject and an object. Therefore the subject "changes his mind" about the object in the context of the sentence.

In the Bible metanoeo is related to the salvation of the unbeliever. The unbeliever is the subject and the object is God, usually the Lord Jesus Christ. The unbeliever, after hearing the gospel, "changes his mind" about the Lord Jesus Christ. The verb metanoeo, when in reference to salvation, does not mean "repentance" toward sin.

The verb metanoeo has no emotional connotation. The Greek verb metamelomai is also translated "repent," and it does have an emotional connotation of regret and feeling sorry for something the subject has done; but this verb is not used in regards to salvation. The Critical Lexicon & Concordance to the English & Greek New Testament by E.W. Bullinger says metamelomai means "to rue, regret; to have dissatisfaction with one's self for what one has done, to change or alter one's purpose, have anxiety consequent on a past transaction; to have pain of mind, rather than change of mind; and change of purpose, rather than change of heart." The Theological Dictionary of the New Testament says, "[Metanoia] [repentance, the noun form of metanoeo) means a change of heart either generally or in respect of a specific sin, whereas [metamelomai] means `to experience remorse.' [Metanoia] implies that one has later arrived at a different view of something, [metamelomai] that one has a different feeling about."

Why I say that metanoeo does not mean "repentance toward sin" is also simple. An unbeliever cannot turn from his sin and stop sinning. It is impossible. Only after one becomes a believer does that person have the ability to turn from sin. Salvation must come first before we can "repent" and have the power to "turn from your sins." We are not freed from the power of sin until we are saved.

> Because the mind set on the flesh is hostile toward God; for it does not subject itself to the law of God, for it is not even able to do so; and those who are in the flesh cannot please God (Rom. 8:7-8, italics added).

> For if we have become united with Him in the likeness of his death, . . . knowing this, that our old self was crucified with Him, that our body of sin might be done away with, that we should no longer be slaves to sin; for he who has died is freed from [the power of] sin (Rom. 6:5-7).

> Now those who belong to Christ Jesus have crucified the flesh with its passions and desires. But now faith has come, we are no longer under a tutor (Gal. 5:24-25).

> But I say, walk by the Spirit, and you will not carry out the desires of the flesh. For the flesh sets its desire against the

Spirit, and the Spirit against the flesh; for these are in opposition to one another, so that you may not do the things that you please. But if you are led by the Spirit, you are not under the Law (Gal. 5:16-18).

And the Law came in that the transgression might increase (Rom. 5:20).

For if a law had been given which was able to impart life, then righteousness would indeed have been based on law. Therefore the Law has become our tutor to lead us to Christ, that we may be justified by faith (Gal. 3:21, 24).

Whatever is not from faith is sin (Rom. 14:23).

Even so Abraham believed God, and it was reckoned to him as righteousness (Gal. 3:6).

What do you put your faith in? Turning from sin or turning to Christ? The change of mind is about Christ since He is the door to salvation. Turning from sin is about the law; no person has ever been able to completely stop sinning because the law is still active, which increases sin.

Salvation is "faith alone, in Christ alone, by grace alone." Salvation is 100 percent by God and a free gift from God. God gets all the credit for salvation. Therefore repentance cannot be added to salvation. If repentance of man is added then man gets part of the credit for salvation; this would violate the truth of salvation being 100 percent by God. Salvation is 100 percent from the grace of God.

Repentance is man's part of salvation. Repentance is making the choice to have a relationship with God. Repentance is changing one's mind, not about sin, but about Jesus Christ. Sin is not the issue because Jesus Christ paid the penalty for every sin that has been committed or will be committed. Therefore Jesus Christ, not sin, is the issue involved in having peace with God.

Believing is God's part of salvation. Man believes by faith in the promise of God that he will be saved because of what Jesus did on the cross. God the Father gets the credit for providing the way of salvation. God the Son Jesus get the credit for executing the plan by coming to earth as a human and dying on the cross to satisfy God's righteousness and justice as the substitute for the believer. In response to the faith of a believer, God imputes His righteousness to the believer, and therefore the believer is saved from the wrath of God; God again gets the credit.

The Bible does not say to "repent of your sins and turn from your sins" to be saved. The Bible says to "believe in the work of Jesus Christ" for salvation. Reconciliation with God comes not from turning from sin but from the work of Jesus Christ on the cross. The spiritual death of Jesus Christ on the cross satisfied the holiness of God. This is called propitiation. God's righteousness and justice were satisfied by Christ's payment for the sins of the whole world. Jesus Christ and His work on the cross is what people have to change their minds about to receive salvation and be reconciled to God.

If repentance means "turning from your sins" the result would be complete by the act of "now doing that particular sin" again. But in Matthew 3:8 "Therefore bring forth fruit in keeping with repentance;" Fruit does not come from ending a sinning behavior. Repentance is a changed life with evidence of fruit. Repentance is turning to God, loving Him for who He is and what He has done and serving Him under the power of the Holy Spirit, there by producing fruit.

The verses that best reveal this truth: Hebrews 7:18-25 **For, on the one had, there is a setting aside of a former command-ment because of its weakness and uselessness (for the Law made nothing perfect), and on the other hand there is a bringing in of a better hope, through which we draw near to God. Jesus has become the guarantee of a better covenant. Hence, also, He is able to save forever those who draw near to God through Him, since He always lives to make intercession for them.**

This verse says to draw near to God through Jesus Christ. This verse does not mention sin or turning away from. The people that draw near to God through Jesus Christ and His work on the cross are saved forever. The law concerning sin make nothing and no one perfect; drawing near to God through Jesus Christ makes one perfect and declared righteous by God.

Why Is This Important?

This is important because salvation is a legal transaction between God and the believer, a covenant between God and the believer. In the final judgment in God's court for believers, this covenant with God is the evidence presented that shows that the payment for the sins of this believer have been "paid in full"; therefore the believer will be found innocent and not suffer the wrath of God in eternal separation from God. Salvation is an unmerited free gift from God by His grace to everyone who believes.

Is It Necessary to "Feel Sorry" for Sins?

As mentioned above, the Greek word metamelomai connotes regret and feeling sorry for sins. Metamelomai is an emotional repentance of the wrongdoer who is desperately sorrowful. Some believers truly feel sorrow for sin. It is not wrong to feel sorry for sin. However, the emotional repentance is incompatible and not part of the grace system of forgiveness prescribed by God. Therefore, feeling sorry for sin gains no merit from God for the repentant believer. Some believers are emotional and in their response to forgiveness and cleansing by God, their gratitude is demonstrated by an emotional response. Again, it gains no merit from God because God looks 100 percent on what Jesus did on the cross. Jesus' work on the cross satisfied God's requirement for forgiveness, so the emotional response from a believer has no value to God.

Therefore a believer does not have to feel sorry for his sin, apologize for his sin, show remorse for his sin, punish himself for his sin, or promise to not sin again in order to get forgiveness. The only thing necessary for forgiveness is confession and acknowledgment of the sin by a believer. God wants the believer to agree with Him that he sinned against heaven and God.

Judgment of Unbelievers

Like most other mathematicians, when I have trouble solving a complex problem, if possible I start with the answer and work backwards. In this way I can gain wisdom about the problem so that I can ultimately find the solution in a straightforward manner. Let's do the same with salvation. This means examining the judgment of someone who does not receive salvation. By seeing what they are judged for, we can see what they should have done to receive salvation.

> He who does not believe the Son shall not see life, but the wrath of God abides on him (John 3:36).

> He who does not believe has been judged already, because he has not believed in the name of the only begotten Son of God (John 3:18).

Man's Approach to God

- Some people deny the existence of God.
- Some people acknowledge God but deny the need to have a relationship with Him.
- Some people create their own way to have a relationship with God.
- Some people attempt to live by the law to gain the approbation of God.
- Some people believe that being a good person will satisfy the requirements of God for a relationship with Him.

> There is a way that seems right to man, but its end is death (Prov. 14:12).

The gospel is the good news of how to approach God and receive His salvation. God is holy and cannot have anything to do with anyone who is not holy. All people are sinners and are therefore unholy and separated from God. Man's approach to God falls short.

But God provides a way for man to have a relationship with Him. God sent His only begotten Son, Jesus Christ, to pay the penalty of man's sins. Jesus arose from the dead and is now seated at the right hand of God. Every person who believes that Jesus Christ died as his substitute on the cross and arose from the dead shall be saved.

> How I did not shrink from declaring to you anything that was profitable, and teaching you publicly and from house to house, solemnly testifying to both Jews and Greeks of repentance toward God and faith in our Lord Jesus Christ (Acts 20:20-21).

This verse clearly states that repentance is "toward God" and not "away from sin." Their repentance is from being independent of God and not having a need for God. Their repentance is about not coming to God on His terms.

A person repents by "changing his mind" about his approach to God. A person repents by acknowledging that he needs God and that his approach to God in the past has fallen short. Repentance is a person "changing his mind" about his approach to God and deciding to choose Jesus Christ and His work on the cross as his approach to God, which is God's prescribed way.

Salvation is when a person believes in his heart on Jesus Christ, Jesus' death on the cross, and Jesus' resurrection from the dead.

Believing on Jesus Christ is a non-meritorious action. The object of belief gets the credit for the act, not the one doing the act of believing.

Romans 1:17 reveals that the "righteousness of God is a righteousness that God provides for people on the basis of and in response to faith in the gospel. Such a righteousness is totally unachievable by human efforts.

Important Thoughts on Salvation and Living the Christian Life

In response to faith, this righteousness is imputed by God in justification and imparted progressively in regeneration and sanctification, culminating in glorification, when standing and state become identical. To justify a person is to declare him legally righteousness.

The first step in the revelation of the righteousness that God provides for people by faith is to set forth their need for it because they are under God's judgment. The human race stands condemned and helpless apart from God's grace. God never condemns anyone without just cause.

The revealing of the wrath of God is an expression of His personal righteousness and its opposition to human sinfulness (Rom. 1:18). God's wrath is directed against all the godlessness and wickedness of men, not against men as such. God hates sin and judges it, but He loves sinners and desires their salvation.

Knowledge concerning God is available to all (Rom. 1:19-20). This knowledge is called natural revelation because it is seen in the created world and is accessible to the entire human race. God has made it plain. God is Spirit and therefore invisible to the physical eyes. In a physical sense, His qualities can be understood by the human mind only as reflected in what has been made; that is, in God's creative work. Divine nature embraces the properties that make God God. Creation, which people see, reveals God's character as the all-powerful deity.

People are without excuse. Their refusal to acknowledge and glorify God leads to a downward spiral: first, worthless thinking; next, moral insensitivity; and then the religious stupidity of idol worship.

The truth is that people are creatures of God and can find true fulfillment only in worshiping and obediently serving God the Creator. Yet, people believe the lie that the creature (angelic or human) can exist independent of God, self-sufficient, self-directing, and self-fulfilling. Mankind has made himself his own gods in place of the true God (Rom. 1:22-23).

As a result, God gave them over to shameful lusts, passions of disgust and disgrace. Sex within marriage is a holy gift from God, but otherwise sex is impurity and the using of bodies contrary to God's intent.

The whole pattern of evil becomes the lifestyle of people who continue to do these very things in open defiance of God, a defiance aggravated by fully knowing that these things deserve death and yet encouraging others in the same lifestyle (Rom. 1:32). Such extremity of human rebellion against God fully warrants God's condemnation.

Everyone in the entire human race has turned away from God and commits sins even though there are differences of frequency, extent, and degree. All are without excuse and without escape. The sin that separates us from God is unbelief.

God's wrath against people's sins is being stored up like a great reservoir until the day when it will all be poured forth in His righteous judgment. On that day God will give to each person according to what he has done. God's judgment will be based on the standard of truth, and it will be impartial (Rom. 2:5-6).

God bestows eternal life on those who have placed their faith in Jesus Christ. On the other hand, wrath and anger will be the portion of the self-seeking, who reject the truth and follow evil. Each one who does evil will receive trouble and distress. It is a just recompense of God (Rom. 2:7-11).

A person's habitual conduct, whether good or evil, reveals the condition of his heart. Eternal life is not rewarded for good living (which is works) but is God's grace to those who believe.

Conscience is an important part of human nature, but it is not an absolutely trustworthy indicator of what is right. One's conscience can be good, clear, guilty, corrupted, weak, or seared. All people need to trust the Lord Jesus Christ so that the blood of Christ might cleanse their conscience.

The righteous judgment of God is an essential ingredient of the gospel.

God's absolute standards are known. God punishes the wicked and rewards the righteous impartially, according to their works, which reveals their hearts.

No one on his or her own can be declared righteous by God. God declares a person righteous at the moment of salvation when the person believes on the Lord Jesus Christ and his work on the cross. No one's good works will earn that person a declaration of righteousness by God.

Apart from the indwelling Holy Spirit, people cannot exhibit the fruit of the Spirit (Gal 5:22). They have no inner spiritual capacity whereby they can normally and automatically exercise genuine kindness toward others. Instead, sin causes them to be selfish and self-centered. There is no fear of God before their eyes.

The law is not a way for a person to be declared righteous (justi-fied) in God's sight. The law was given so that through it we become conscious of sin. The law is an instrument of condemnation.

In God's condemnation of the human race, His own personal, infinite righteousness was revealed along with the fact that not a single human being (except Jesus) has ever or will ever be able to meet that standard and be accepted by God on his own merit.

Since the entire human race was plunged into sin with Adam, all are sinners. Not only have all sinned, but also all fall short (Rom. 3:23). The simple fact is that as a sinner not a single human being by his own efforts is able to measure up to the glory of God. God's glory is His splendor, the outward manifestation of His attributes. God desires that humans share that splendor, that they become like Him, that is, Christlike. Yet their sin keeps them from sharing it.

God's justification to those who believe is provided freely, as a free gift without charge, by His grace (Rom. 3:24). But God would not declare a person righteous without an objective basis, without dealing with his sin. That basis is the redemption that came by Christ Jesus. Redemption is a ransom payment.

The death of Christ on the cross of Calvary was the price for human sin. It secured release from the bondage of Satan and sin for every person who trusts God's promise of forgiveness and salva-tion. We trust God's promise, not our decision to turn from sin, for salvation.

God presents Christ, as the sacrifice of atonement (Rom. 3:25). Atonement is propitiation. The mercy seat is the place of atonement in the tabernacle's ark of the covenant. There a bull's blood was sprinkled on the Day of Atonement to cover (atone) Israel's sins and satisfy God for another year. Jesus' death is the final sacrifice that completely satisfied God's demands against sinful people, thus averting His wrath from those who believe.

By the death of Jesus and the shedding of His blood the penalty for sin has been paid and God has been satisfied, or propitiated. A believer places his faith in Jesus. Thus, he appropriates by faith the atoning work of Christ.

God demonstrates His justice, His own judicial righteousness, because in his own forbearance (holding back, delay) He had left the sins committed before unpunished. God anticipated His provision for sins in the death of Jesus Christ.

God's purpose in the redemptive and propitiatory death of Jesus Christ was that He could be seen to be just and the one who justifies, the One who declares righteous the one who has faith in Jesus (Rom. 3:26). God's divine dilemma was how to satisfy His own righteousness and its demands against sinful people and at the same time demonstrate His grace, love, and mercy to restore rebellious, alienated creatures to Himself. The solution was the sacrifice of Jesus Christ, God's incarnate Son, and the acceptance by faith of that provision by individual sinners. Christ's death vindicated God's own righteousness (He is just because sin was "paid for") and enables God to declare every believing sinner righteous.

Therefore the promise comes by faith so that it may be by grace. Responding in faith to God's promise is not meritorious, since the promise springs from His grace, His disposition of favor toward those who deserve his wrath. The human exercise of faith is simply the prerequisite response of trust in God and His promise.

Because of the sinner's response by faith to Christ's sacrifice on the cross, God has declared him righteous. Believers will never be condemned to hell or be objects of God's coming tribulation wrath.

The law was added so that the trespass might increase, and as a result, God's grace might abound (Rom. 5:20). In no way is the abundance of God's grace designed to encourage sin, however.

The fact is Christians have "died to sin" (Rom. 6:2). The Greek aorist tense for "died" suggests a specific point when the action occurred—at salvation. Death, whether physical or spiritual, means separation, not extinction. Death to sin is separation from sin's power, not the extinction of sin. Being dead to sin means being "set free from sin."

Sanctification begins with regeneration, the implanting of spiritual life in the believer. From that starting point, sanctification is God's work of progressively separating a believer from sin to Himself and transforming his total life experience toward holiness and purity, conforming to the likeness of God's Son.

The first attitude for sanctification demanded of believers is to "count" themselves dead to sin but alive to God in Christ Jesus (Rom. 6:11). Being able to reckon something as true, however, depends on knowing and believing certain things. Our "old self" was crucified with Christ and united with Him in His death so that the body of sin might be rendered powerless (Rom. 6:6). This means that before his conversion one's physical body is controlled or ruled by sin. But at salvation the power of controlling sin is broken; it is rendered powerless or ineffective.

Anyone who has died has been freed from sin (Rom. 6:7). The words "freed from sin" are essentially equivalent to "has been justified" or "declared righteous." The perfect tense of this verb describes a past action with a continuing effect or force. Sin no longer has the legal right to force its mastery and control on a believer, for he has died with Christ. Christians are to count themselves dead to (in reference to) sin but alive to God. Since they are dead to its power, they ought to recognize that fact and not continue to sin. They are to realize that they have new life in Christ; they share His resurrection life.

The attitude of mind that a believer has died to sin must be translated into action in his experience. Paul commanded, therefore, "Do not let sin reign" as it did before salvation (Rom. 6:12). The present imperative negative can also be translated, "Stop letting sin reign." When sin reigns in people's lives and bodies, they obey its evil desires. Sin enslaves, making a person subject to his own desires. Sin manifests itself through one's physical actions in this body.

Paul's command was to not offer the parts of our bodies as instruments or weapons of wickedness or unrighteousness. Present once and for all ourselves to God and our bodies as instruments of righteousness (Rom. 6:13).

God's design is that sin not be our master. The reason this should not happen is that we are not under law but under grace (Rom. 6:14). The power of sin is the law. If believers were still under the law, it would be impossible to keep sin from exercising mastery. But since believers are under grace, this can be done by following Paul's instructions.

The wages of sin is death (Rom. 6:23). This death is eternal separation from God in hell, in which unbelievers suffer conscious torment forever. This is the wages they have earned and deserve because of their sin. By contrast, the gift of God is eternal life. Eternal life is a gift that cannot be earned.

It is one thing for a believer to understand that his identification with Jesus Christ means that he has died to sin and that he should count or reckon that to be true. But it is something else for him to deal with the sin nature that remains within and its efforts to express itself in his thoughts and actions. This is the internal conflict in the area of sanctification that every believer faces.

In Romans 10:9 confessing with the mouth that Jesus is Lord is mentioned first in order to conform to the order of the quotation from Deuteronomy 30:14. The confession is an acknowledgment that God has been incarnated in Jesus, that Jesus Christ is God. Also essential is heart-faith that God raised Him from the dead. The result is salvation. The true order is given in verse 10: it is with your heart that you believe and are justified, and it is with your mouth that you confess and are saved. It is confessed unto salvation. Yet these are not two separate steps to salvation. They are chronologically together. Salvation comes through acknowledging to God that Christ is God and believing in Him.

Everyone who calls on the name of the Lord will be saved (Rom. 10:13). To call on the Lord means to pray in faith for salvation.

A believer's offering of his total life as a sacrifice to God is sacred service (Rom. 12:1). Such an offering is holy and pleasing to God. It is spiritual worship, referring to any ministry performed for God, such as that of the priests and the Levites. Such an offering is obviously a desirable response for believers.

Living according to the lifestyle of the present evil age must now be put aside (Rom. 12:2). We must be transformed and keep on being transformed by the renewing of our mind. This is a total change from the inside out. The key to this change is the mind, the control center of one's attitudes, thoughts, feelings, and actions. As one's mind keeps on being made new by the spiritual input of God's Word, prayer, and Christian fellowship, his lifestyle keeps on being transformed.

Do not be proud or think too highly of yourself. Do not be conceited; it is an attitude that makes empathy impossible.

The Gospel (Paul's presentation in Romans)

1. Romans 1:16: *"For I am not ashamed of the gospel, for it is the power of God for salvation to every one who believes."*
2. Romans 1:17: *"The righteous man shall live by faith."*
3. Romans 1:18-20: "For the wrath of God is revealed from heaven against all ungodliness and unrighteousness of men . . . because that which is known about God is evident with them. For since the creation of the world, His invisible attributes, His eternal power and divine nature, have been clearly seen . . . so that they are without excuse."
4. Romans 1:21-31: *"For even though they knew God, they did not honor Him as God . . .*
   A. [They] exchanged the glory of the incorruptible God for an image in the form of corruptible man. God gave them over in the lusts of their hearts to impurity. . . .
   B. [They] worshiped and served the creature rather than the Creator. . . . God gave them over to degrading passions. . . .
   C. Just as they did not see fit to acknowledge God any longer, God gave them over to a depraved mind, ... being filled with . . . greed, evil; full of envy, murder, strife, deceit, malice; they are gossips, slanderers, haters of God, insolent, arrogant, boastful, inventors of evil, disobedient to parents, . . . untrustworthy, unloving, unmerciful."
5. Romans 1:32: *"Although they know the ordinance of God, that those who practice such things are worthy of death."*
6. Romans 2:5-6: *"Because of your stubbornness and unrepentant heart you are storing up wrath for yourself in the*

day of wrath and revelation of the righteous judgment of God, who will render to each person according to his deeds:

   A. to those who by perseverance in doing good seek for glory and honor and immortality, eternal life;

   B. but to those who are selfishly ambitious and do not obey the truth, but obey unrighteousness, wrath and indignation.

7. Romans 2:16: *"God will judge the secrets of men through Christ Jesus."*

8. Romans 3:21-26: *"But now the righteousness of God has been manifested, the righteousness of God through faith in Jesus Christ for all those who believe . . . being justified as a gift by His grace through the redemption which is in Christ Jesus, ... whom God displayed publicly as a propitiation in His blood through faith. This was to demonstrate His righteousness, ... that He might be just and the justifier of the one who has faith in Jesus."*

9. Romans 4:5: *"But to the one who does not work, but believes in Him who justifies the ungodly, his faith is reckoned as righteousness."*

10. Romans 5:1: *"Therefore, having been justified by faith, we have peace with God through our Lord Jesus Christ."*

11. Romans 5:8: *"God demonstrates His own love toward us, in that while we were yet sinners, Christ died for us."*

12. Romans 5:9: *"Having now been justified by His blood, we shall be saved from the wrath of God through Him."*

13. Romans 6:5-7, 19, 22: *"For if we have become united with Him in the likeness of His death, ... our old self was crucified with Him, ... we should no longer be slaves to sin; for he who has died is freed from* [power of] *sin. . . . Now present your members as slaves to righteousness, resulting in sanctification. ... and the outcome, eternal life."*

14. Romans 6:23: *"For the wages of sin is death, but the free gift of God is eternal life in Christ Jesus our Lord."*

15. Romans 8:32: *"He who did not spare His own Son, but delivered Him up for us all, how will He not also with Him freely give us all things?"*
16. Romans 9:16: *"So then it does not depend on the man who wills or the man who runs, but on God who has mercy."*
17. Romans 10:9-13: *"If you confess with your mouth Jesus as Lord, and believe in your heart that God raised Him from the dead, you shall be saved; for with the heart man believes, resulting in righteousness, and with the mouth he confesses, resulting in salvation. For whoever will call upon the name of the Lord will be saved."*
18. Romans 10:17: *"So faith comes by hearing, and hearing by the word of Christ."*
19. Romans 11:29: *"The gifts and the calling of God are irrevocable."*
20. Romans 12:1-2: *"Present your bodies a living and holy sacrifice, acceptable to God, which is your spiritual service of worship. And do not be conformed to this world but be transformed by the renewing of your mind."*

Summary

God desires to have a personal relationship with all His creatures. God loves you and desires to establish a relationship with you. God has provided the means for you to have that relationship with Him. Your sin, which comes from the old sin nature you were born with, has separated you from God. But God loves you and has provided a way to bridge the gap that separates you from Him. That bridge is Jesus Christ. God sent Jesus here to pay the penalty for your sins. Jesus did that by dying on the cross. Jesus rose again, ascended into heaven, and now sits at the right hand of God. God wants a relationship with you. All you need to do is accept His free gift of salvation and become a child of God.

Salvation is by faith alone, by grace alone, by Jesus Christ's work on the cross alone, by the choosing of God the Father alone and by the power of the Holy Spirit alone. That describes God's part. Our part is to simply believe the gospel as proclaimed by God in the

Bible. When we believe, God does the rest. The object of our belief receives the credit, not us. Each member of the Godhead is involved in salvation and alone receives the credit. We receive what is given to us. We receive it by grace because we don't deserve it. It is a free gift and deserves our eternal gratitude.

Again, salvation is by faith alone, by Christ alone, by grace alone, by God and the Holy Spirit alone. This is the door into the kingdom of God.

Maybe you find yourself today not knowing whether you have an eternal relationship with God or not. Maybe you've not in the kingdom of God.

You may not know whether you are going to spend eternity in heaven or not. I have good news for you. <u>You can change this right now.</u> You can become a child of God in the next couple of minutes and have an eternal father-child relationship with Him.

Do the following, and you can become a child of God.

- Believe that God created you and loves you.
- Acknowledge that you've made bad choices and sinned against Him.
- Believe that Jesus died and paid the penalty for all your sins.
- Turn to God and Talk to God; tell Him that you know you've sinned and that you accept Jesus' payment for your sins.

You are now a child of God. You have an everlasting relationship with God. Nothing now can separate you from God or the love of God.

Reread this chapter. Think about the decision you just made. Now, tell someone what you've done and about your decision. Go to a church, and make a public profession of your relationship with God. Get a Bible, and start reading it. God wants you to get to know Him and His plans for you and your future. Join a Bible-believing church, and start hanging out with fellow children of God. God wants you to have an abundant life. This is the first step toward that end.

CHAPTER 7

Restoring Fellowship with God

In a previous chapter the parable of the prodigal son was interpreted from the point of view that the two sons were both believers
struggling to live the spiritual life. It was noted that the younger son
lived a carnal life and was carrying out the desires of his flesh in his
actions and behaviors. The older son also was living a carnal life as
seen by his outburst of anger, jealousy, and envy. Later, the younger
son repented and turned from his sin back to God. The older son did
not repent. The older son's sins were all attitude sins of the heart, but
they were still deeds of the flesh. When a believer is living a carnal
life, he is out of fellowship with God.

A believer is always in one of two states—living a spiritual
lifestyle or living a carnal lifestyle. A believer is spiritual when he
living under the control of the Holy Spirit. When a believer sins,
he becomes carnal and loses fellowship with God. So how does a
person become spiritual again after sinning? The answer is found in
what I call the "restoration process."

Why Be Filled with The Holy Spirit?

Romans 14:17-18 *for the kingdom of God is not eating and
drinking, but righteousness and peace and joy in the Holy Spirit.
For he who in this way serves Christ is acceptable to God and
approved by men.*

John 16:7,13 *"But I tell you the truth, it is to your advantage that I go away; for if I do not go away, the Helper shall not come to you; but if I go, I will send Him to you. But when He, the Spirit of truth comes, He will guide you into all the truth.*

1 Corinthians 12:7, 11, 18 *But to each one is given the manifestation of the Spirit for the common good. But one and he same Spirit works all these things, distributing to each one individually just as He wills. But now God has placed the members, each one of them, in the body, just as He desired.*

Epheasians 4:11-12 *And He [The Holy Spirit] gave some as apostles, and some as prophets, and some as evangelists, and some as pastors and teachers, for the equipping of the saints for the work of service to the building up of the body of Christ;*

The Holy Spirit provides the power and knowledge to serve Christ. Each believer is given spiritual gift(s) for service according to the desires of the Holy Spirit. Every believer is important to the functioning of the body of Christ in the kingdom of God. God has a plan for each believer and God has provided the means and the power to execute His plan. The believer has that power when he is filled with the Holy Spirit.

Important Questions Raised by the Parable

What Is the Difference Between Being Spiritual and Being Carnal?

When a Christian is in control of his own life, he is a carnal believer. When a Christian is filled with the Spirit and under control of the Spirit, he is spiritual and in fellowship with God. Carnality began with Eve, when she was deceived by the subtle suggestion that she could be as smart as God—and therefore independent—if she ate of the Tree of the Knowledge of Good and Evil. The acronym S-I- N, for Selfish Independent Nature, is an appropriate description of sin. A person is either 100 percent spiritual or 100 percent carnal. A person is either dependent upon God and allowing Him to control his life, or a person is independent of God and allowing his old sin nature to have control of his life.

What Happens When a Christian Sins?

When a Christian sins, he is taking control of his life away from God and returning to his former state of being in control of his own life. When a Christian sins, he is back under the control and domination of the old sin nature. Carnality is the status of being out of fellowship with God because of un-confessed sin in the Christian's life. In carnality the Christian loses the filling of the Holy Spirit, which grieves the Spirit. The "filling of the Holy Spirit" means being controlled by the Holy Spirit. Once a person is saved, that person is indwelt by the Holy Spirit forever. When a person sins and become carnal again, he takes control back of his life and therefore no longer filled with the Holy Spirit.

How Does Sin Affect the Christian's Relationship with God?

When a Christian sins, he loses fellowship with God. He does not lose his salvation, for nothing can separate him from a relationship with God. When a person believes in the Lord Jesus Christ, the person becomes a child of God, and God establishes an eternal relationship with that person. When a Christian sins, the Holy Spirit does not leave; rather, the Holy Spirit is "grieved" to lose control of the believer.

How Does a Christian Restore His Fellowship with God?

God provides a way for the Christian who has sinned to restore his relationship with God. The way to restore fellowship with God is by confessing one's sins. When a Christian confesses his sins, God immediately forgives him of his sin, restores fellowship with him, and fills him again with the Spirit.

When we confess our sins, God blots them out and erases them from His memory.

What Does God Do if a Christian Does Not Restore His Fellowship with God?

If a Christian continues in sin, then God disciplines that person. God disciplines the person because He loves the person.

Believer's Fellowship with God

Before a person believes on the Lord Jesus Christ, he is spiritually dead. He does not have a relationship with God or any fellowship with God. The instant a person believes on Jesus Christ he becomes a child of God, is filled with the Spirit, and is brought into fellowship with God.

When a believer sins, he loses fellowship with God and the filling of the Spirit, and thus control by the Spirit. When a believer sins, he does not lose his salvation or his relationship with God.

When a person believes on Jesus Christ and becomes a Christian, he still has the old sin nature he was born with. Therefore, the believer continues to sin. As 1 John 1:8 says, *"If we say that we have no sin, we are deceiving ourselves, and the truth is not in us."* But when a person believes on Jesus Christ, all his sins are forgiven up to that point in his life. When a person sins, he must confess that sin in order to be forgiven that sin. Jesus' death on the cross paid the price so that all the sins can be forgiven. Sins are forgiven when confessed.

The Restoration Process

The divine solution for recovering fellowship with God is by confessing one's sins. First John 1:9 tells us, *"If we confess our sins, He is faithful and righteous to forgive us our sins and to cleanse us from all unrighteousness."* Our sins were all judged when Jesus died on the cross. In dealing with our sins, God sees Jesus' substitutionary sacrifice for us on the cross. God forgives the person's sin at salvation because of Jesus' death on the cross. God also forgives a believer his sins when he confesses them. When the believer confesses his sin, God forgives him, restores fellowship with him, and fills him with the Spirit.

Doctrine of Repentance (after salvation)

As we saw in the last chapter, the Greek verb metanoeo, translated "repent," means a complete change of mind and always involves a change for the better. As a transitive verb metanoeo must have a subject and an object. Thus, the subject "changes his mind" about the object in the context of the sentence.

Repentance involves a change of mind—waking up to reality, seeing things as they really are, and recognizing the error of your ways—resulting in a change of action. To repent means to change. Repentance is a change of thinking that results in a change of life. Repentance includes forsaking old patterns, habits, and priorities, and all things that have controlled you.

Repentance after salvation does means "changing your mind about sin." God is holy and desires for believers to be holy also. God tells the believer to not let sin reign in his body (Rom. 6:11-12) but rather to present his body in righteousness to God, resulting in sanctification, which is spiritual maturity (Rom. 7:19b). A person does not have to repent regarding sin in order to receive salvation, but immediately following salvation he does need to repent and turn away from sin. Only when a person is filled with the Holy Spirit does he have the power in order to turn away from sin. Man alone does not have the power to stop sinning. No one has enough "will power" to stop sinning. A person needs the power of the Holy Spirit in order to not sin.

At the moment of salvation a believer receives the Holy Spirit. With the help of the Holy Spirit a believer has the power to overcome sin. A person cannot turn from his sin until he has received the Holy Spirit. Therefore, a person cannot turn from his sin until after salvation. Consequently, if people are asked to "repent and turn from their sin" in order to be saved, no one could be saved because no one has the power to turn from his sin until he is saved and receives the

Holy Spirit. Repentance for salvation, therefore, is changing one's mind toward God and believing God for providing salvation. All it takes for salvation is belief in God. A person does not have to do anything but make a choice and believe.

Doctrine of Divine Discipline for Believers

Divine discipline is punitive action from God for believers (and believers only) who continue in sin. Hebrews 12:11 explains, *"All discipline for the moment seems not to be joyful, but sorrowful; yet to those who have been trained by it, afterwards it yields the peaceful fruit of righteousness."*

Divine Condemnation for Rejection of Jesus

Unbelievers receive their discipline in the final judgment, which is eternal separation from God in hell. Paul wrote, *"But because of your stubbornness and unrepentant heart you are storing up wrath for yourself in the day of wrath and revelation of the righteous judgment of God, who will render to every man according to his deeds"* (Rom. 1:5-6).

Condemnation is simply the end result of the rejection of Jesus Christ as Savior. Jesus said, *"For the mouth speaks out of that which fills the heart. . . . I tell you that every careless word that people speak, they shall give an accounting for it in the day of judgment"* (Matt. 12:34, 36).

Can a Person Stop Sinning?

As the following verses demonstrate, the believer is freed from the power of sin. And while a state of sinlessness cannot be attained in this life (1 John 1:8), the believer has the power to control the old sin nature if he chooses to do so by being under the control of the Holy Spirit.

Knowing this, that our old self was crucified with Him, that our body of sin might be done away with, that we should no longer be a slave to sin; for he who has died is freed from [the power of] sin (Rom. 6:6-7).

For sin shall not be master over you, for you are not under law, but under grace. . . . So now present your members as slaves to righteousness, resulting in sanctification [the process of becoming more like Christ]. . . . But now, having been freed from sin and enslaved to God, you derive your benefit, resulting in sanctification, and the outcome, eternal life (Rom. 6:14, 19, 22).

For that which I am doing, I do not understand; for I am not practicing what I would like to do, but I am doing the very thing I hate. . . . So now, no longer am I the done doing it, but sin [old sin nature] *which indwells me. . . . I find then the principle that evil* [old sin nature] *is present in me, the one who wishes to do good* (Rom. 7:15, 17, 21).

For the law of the Spirit of life in Christ Jesus has set you free from the law of sin and of death (Rom. 8:2).

As obedient children, do not be conformed to the former lusts which were yours in your ignorance, but like the Holy One who called you, be holy yourselves also in all your behavior; because it is written, "You shall be holy, for I am holy" (1 Pet. 1:14-16).

He Himself bore our sins in His body on the cross, that we might die to sin and live to righteousness; for by His wounds you were healed (1 Pet. 2:24).

Again, repentance is turning to God. Romans 5:20 explains the law of sin, *"and the Law came in that the transgression might increase."* Romans 8:2 contains the explanation for overcoming sin in our life. The old sin nature in a person by law is going to continually motivate a person to sin. To stop sinning a person must repent and turn to God and away from self, which tries to stop sinning via will power, ego strength and other man derived methods. When we live with the Spirit in control of our lives, the Law of the Spirit gives to us the power for us to not sin. Again, God provides for all our needs (Philippians 4:19); here, our need is to have the power to stop sinning. We can't do it on our own, we need God's help to stop sinning. Repentance is turning away from self (by crucifying self) to God for power in order to not continue in sin.

For example, if I make a resolution to have more self-control which is one of the fruit of the Spirit (Galatians 5:22-23). This becomes a commandment, which actually increase sin. So the harder I try on my own for self-control then the more I will fail to have self-control. To gain self-control, I have to confess this sin to God by acknowledging I don't have self-control, and then asking Christ to live in me and give me the power to have self-control. When I do this, then I will have self-control.

Repentance for salvation is turning to God for salvation and accepting Christ's death as payment for your sins. Repentance for restoration of a carnal lifestyle is turning to God for restoration and accepting Christ's living in you to give you power over sin.

Doctrine of Eternal Security

In Romans 8:38-39, Paul wrote, *"For I am convinced that neither death, nor life, nor angels, nor principalities, nor things present, nor things to come, nor powers, nor height, nor depth, nor any other created thing, shall be able to separate us from the love of God, which is in Christ Jesus our Lord."* The apostle understood the doctrine of eternal security—that God not only saves but also securely keeps those He saves.

The believer is held by Jesus' hand, and Jesus will never let go. The Lord Himself said, *"And I give eternal life to them, and they shall never perish; and no one shall snatch them out of My hand"* (John 10:28).

Doctrine of God's Plan of Salvation and His Direction and Provision for the Christian Life

1. A person hears the gospel (this activates the Holy Spirit).
2. The person changes his mind about God and decides he wants to appropriate the information he has heard in the gospel.
3. The person by faith believes the gospel, the good news that Jesus died on the cross as his substitute, paid the penalty for his sins, and was resurrected from the dead.
4. The person expresses his belief in Jesus Christ in a prayer to God.
5. God in his grace regenerates the person, makes a new creation out of him, and provides the indwelling of the Holy Spirit as a pledge and down payment of the believer's eternal relationship with God.
6. The person confesses with his mouth to someone his belief and his salvation.
7. The person is directed to be baptized to publicly identify himself with Jesus in the likeness of His death on the cross and His resurrection from the dead.
8. The person is directed to begin the inward transformation process of becoming like Jesus Christ. This happens by the renewing of the mind through the daily study and input of Bible doctrine and applying the doctrine by faith. This process of becoming a mature believer continues until the person dies or is taken up in the rapture.
9. The person is directed to gather with other believers to worship God and for fellowship.
10. The person is directed to love the Lord his God with all his heart, mind, soul, and strength. This means continual communication with God through prayer.
11. The person is directed to love his neighbor as himself and to love his enemies.
12. The person is to be aware that the Christian life is difficult because he is going to have temptation to sin, actually sin, experience the consequences of his sin, possibly experience the discipline of God for his continued sin, and go through

undeserved suffering as Christ did. But the new believer is equipped to deal with any and all difficulties of life and can still have joy and peace during the various trials. The believer can have stability despite the adversity he goes through, for God promises to never leave or forsake the believer.

Principles for Believers for Maintaining Spirituality

1. When you sin, confess your sin to God, and He will forgive you and restore you to fellowship with Him (Restoration Process).
2. When you sin expect to receive the natural consequences of your sin.
3. You do not have to feel sorry for your sin, or punish yourself for your sin, or promise to not sin again. God's provision for restored fellowship with Him is for you to confess your sin.
5. When you confess your sin, God forgets your sin; therefore you also can forget and disregard your sin. But beware that God may still allow you to suffer the consequences of your sin.
6. When you don't confess your sins, do not be surprised when you start a downward trend of sinning more and in other areas of your life.
7. When you continue in sin, expect to experience God's discipline. A believer's sin is serious business with God. God resists the proud. God disciplines you because He loves you.
8. When you experience the pain and frustration from God's discipline, immediately follow principle 1—confess your sins.
9. When you sin, do not be surprised when you are inappropriately judged by other carnal believers who are judgmental and self-righteous.
10. If you are being prideful, judgmental, and self-righteous, then immediately follow principle 1. Confess your sins before you experience the discipline of God.

11. Be aware that it is God's intent to conform you to the image of His Son, Jesus Christ.
12. Do not love this world or be conformed to this world, but daily be transforming your mind through the input of God's Word and other positive spiritual material.
13. Being spiritual comes by being controlled by the Holy Spirit. And this comes from being filled with the Spirit by confessing your sins.
14. Don't be deceived by your own pride so that you become arrogant, self-exalting, or haughty in your attitudes.
15. If confronted because of your sin by a spiritual believer, watch the words that come out of your mouth, for they reveal the secrets of the heart and negative thinking.
16. Be aware than emotional remorse is not always sincere and is not a part of God's design for repentance.
17. Don't try to win the approbation of God by doing "good works." Have the right motivation when serving God.

Summary

At salvation, a person becomes a child of God. Once one is a child of God, nothing can change that relationship; a believer always remains a child of God. But sin separates a believer from fellowship with God because the believer is putting "self" back on the throne of his life in place of the Holy Spirit. It grieves the Holy Spirit when the believer removes the Spirit from being in control of his life and returns to his carnal lifestyle.

God wants to have that parent-child relationship with the believer continuously. But the believer has free will and can decide to follow his own will down a separate path from God. When a believer sins, he is back in control of his life, working in his own energies. He does not have the Holy Spirit strengthening, leading, teaching, and comforting him. Repent and turn to God for help.

God makes it easy for the carnal believer to return to fellowship with Him. If you find yourself away from fellowship with God right now, consider what you've lost and the mess your life is in right now. Are you ready to return to God's family and fellowship?

He desires for you to return today. He has made it easy for you to do. Acknowledge all your sins to Him, and He will forgive you and cleanse you from all unrighteousness and restore you to full fellowship with Him. It is really that simple. He can do it because Jesus paid the penalty for all your sins—past, present, and future. Simply acknowledge the sins to Him, and you will be forgiven and restored to fellowship with Him.

You don't have to feel sorry for your sins or promise to not do them again. Agree with Him that you did these sins in the recent past, and He will forgive you, no questions asked.

The same principle is given in Genesis 4:1-7. Cain, Adam and Eve's firstborn, was a tiller of the ground. Able, the second child, was a keeper of flocks. Able brought an offering to the Lord from the firstlings of his flock. Cain brought an offering from the ground. God had regard for Able's offering but not Cain's. Cain became angry, and his countenance fell. God spoke to Cain and set forth a basic principle: *"If you do well, will not your countenance be lifted up? And if you do not do well, sin is crouching at the door; and its desire is for you, but you must master it."* God told him just to do it right the next time and bring an offering from the flock. Then God would have regard for it, and then Cain's countenance would be lifted up.

The choice was Cain's. God wanted him to do it right the next time. God warned him that the temptation to sin is strong, but that he had to master it. God wanted Cain to master it and return to fellowship with God. The same applies to us. God wants us to maintain fellowship with Him.

Aren't you ready to have that fellowship with God again? Aren't you ready to get back to the place that you know that God is hearing and answering your prayers? Aren't you ready to have God's grace and mercy evident in your life again? Aren't you ready again for the Holy Spirit to use you and your spiritual gifts in helping others? Aren't you ready to start pursuing your purpose and doing things that have eternal consequences and rewards? God has provided the way. All you have to decide to do is to agree with Him. He wants to have fellowship with you, His child. Decide now. Act now. Acknowledge your sin; agree with Him. He will forgive you, and you will be back in fellowship with Him. And your countenance, your feelings, will follow your actions and be lifted up. That's a promise!

CHAPTER 8

Religious and Good People

An ancient Greek proverb says, "If you wish to be good, first believe that you are bad." Herein lies the problem for so many "good" and "moral" people—they believe that they are good and acceptable to God just the way they are. And from all outward appearances, they may well be as good, or better, than those who humbly admit their sin and trust in Christ alone for salvation. They are kind to their neighbors, give to good causes, volunteer to help the needy, and even faithfully attend religious services.

People do benefit in tangible ways from the deeds of such good people. There is no denying the fact that many needy, helpless people are healed and cured of disease by the kindness of caring, good people. These people are wonderful and desire praise for their unselfish deeds for the good of humanity. Nevertheless, good people who are without Christ are like the older son in Jesus' parable of the prodigal son. They are religious, good, and moral on the outside but filled with sinful and selfish attitudes on the inside.

Relative Righteousness of Religious, Good, and Moral People

Being a religious, moral, or good person does not make one righteous. The religious, moral, and good person may have a "relative righteousness," much higher than an immoral person or criminal, but that righteousness still falls short of the absolute righteousness of

God. Many people are good, a lot are nice, and some are very good and very moral. Relatively speaking, some people's righteousness is far greater than other people's. But compared to God's standard, every one of these people fall short. Even the extremely religious person with honorable qualities and characteristics falls short of God's absolute righteousness. Jesus said in Matthew 5:20, *"Unless your righteousness surpasses that of the scribes and Pharisees, you shall not enter the kingdom of heaven."*

In His parable of the prodigal son, Jesus was saying that morality and human good is insufficient to have a relationship with God. God is perfectly righteous and cannot fellowship with anyone who is unrighteous.

Religious, moral, and good people in effect are saying either that they need no savior or that they can in some way save themselves. They believe they can satisfy all God's just demands and deliver themselves from the power of sin. However, since all have sinned, it does not matter how moral a person is or how much human good a person does, that person still falls short of the glory of God.

Principles for Religious, Good, and Moral People

There are two overriding biblical principles that relate to religious, good, and moral people who are trusting in themselves rather than Jesus Christ for salvation.

1. Being a moral and good person does not get you into heaven. This amounts to legalism, which is man's futile attempt to gain the approbation of God (salvation) through human works and human good.
2. *You must be born again* (John 3:7). When a person believes in the Lord Jesus Christ and His work on the cross, then the believer is declared righteous. The believer can now have fellowship with God for all eternity.

Summary

Perhaps you are a good person. Maybe you have a generous, sensitive heart and you donate to all the pledge-athons that come on TV asking for donations. Perhaps you give to causes to help the poor, the diseased, and the starving children around the world. Maybe you donate time to work in shelters or other community outreaches to help people in need. Maybe you visit nursing homes and bring joy to needy aging senior citizens. Maybe you volunteer at a children's hospital, giving hope to sick kids dealing with terrible illnesses. Maybe you use your influence and money to champion great humanitarian causes that have a definite effect on the lives of many desperate people.

These are all great things. But there is one problem. Everyone has to come to God on God's terms. If a person were perfect, then all these good deeds might account for something. But no one is perfect; everyone has sinned at least once. And one sin will keep a person from having a relationship with God. In this case, no amount of good can counterbalance the effect of that one sin in God's sight. The good news is that God has made provision to take care of all your sins. He sent Jesus, His Son, to earth to die and pay the penalty for every sin you commit in your entire lifetime. To begin a relationship with God, all you have to do is accept Jesus' payment for your sins instead of depending on your good works.

- Believe that God created you and loves you.
- Acknowledge that you've made bad choices and sinned against Him.
- Believe that Jesus died and paid the penalty for all your sins.
- Tell God you know your good deeds are not enough to get you to heaven and that you are depending on Jesus' payment for your sins to secure the free gift of eternal life from Him. Tell him that you know you've sinned and that you accept Jesus payment for your sins.

If you have done this, you are now a child of God. You have an eternal relationship with God. Nothing now can separate you from God or the love of God.

Perhaps you are a deeply religious or spiritual person. You may be a Sunday school teacher, deacon, priest, pastor, evangelist, prophet or bishop. You may be actively serving God today and changing lives by teaching or preaching the Bible. You may be raising lots of money and helping other Christian ministries serve God in great ways. You may be giving all your time and money to serving God. You may be so religious that people persecute you for it.

These are all great things. But there is one problem. Everyone has to come to God on God's terms. In Psalm 51:16-17 David acknowledged a divine principle: *"For Thou dost not delight in sacrifice, otherwise I would give it; Thou are not pleased with burnt offering. The sacrifices of God are a broken spirit; a broken and contrite heart, O God, Thou will not despise."* Religious things do not save; they are only symbolic of Him who does save. Jesus said, *"And as Moses lifted up the serpent in the wilderness, even so must the Son of Man be lifted up; so that whoever believes will in Him have eternal life. For God so loved the world, that He gave His only begotten Son, that whoever believes in Him should not perish, but have eternal life"* (John 3:14-16).

The only way to have a relationship with God is through His Son, Jesus Christ. Every religious ceremony mentioned in the Bible points to Jesus Christ. Performing religious ceremonies does not save. God requires a broken and contrite heart from everyone who comes to Him. The sacrifices do not save; they are just symbolic. God has made provision for all your sins. He sent Jesus, His Son, to earth to die and pay the penalty for every sin you commit in your entire lifetime. To begin a relationship with God, all you have to do is accept Jesus' payment for your sins instead of depending on your good deeds and religious observance.

- Believe that God created you and loves you.
- Acknowledge that you've made bad choices and sinned against Him.

- Believe that Jesus died and paid the penalty for all your sins.
- Tell God you know your religious deeds are not enough to get you to heaven and that you are depending on Jesus' payment for your sins to secure the free gift of eternal life from Him. Tell him that you know you've sinned and that you accept Jesus payment for your sins.

If you have done this, you are now a child of God. You have an eternal relationship with God. Nothing now can separate you from God or the love of God.

Let's make sure you understand the seriousness of this matter. Unless you have a complete picture of God, you might be tempted to put off this decision. Maybe you were brought up in a good home, had good parents, and you are today an extremely good person. You may not be convinced that you need a savior. Maybe you are an extremely giving and generous person and constantly give considerable gifts to help needy children at home and abroad. Maybe you are famous and rich and don't see the need for a savior. Maybe your personality strengths have taken you far in life, and you don't see your need for a savior. Maybe you think God will take all the above into consideration when you stand before Him and give an account. The prophet Nahum paints an accurate picture of God. "*A jealous and avenging God is the Lord; the Lord is avenging and wrathful. The Lord takes vengeance on His adversaries, and He reserves wrath for His enemies. The Lord is slow to anger and great in power, and the Lord will by no means leave the guilty unpunished. . . . The Lord is good, a stronghold in the day of trouble, and He knows those who take refuge in Him*" (Nah. 1:2-3, 7).

God knows you need the Savior. Those who think they don't need Him are guilty of being God's enemy and will suffer His wrath. Are you sure you don't want to reconsider now your beliefs? God is good; this is true. But it is also true he takes out His wrath on His adversaries and does not leave the guilty unpunished. If you don't want to have any regrets, look again at what you must do to begin a relationship with God. Become a friend of God as you express your need for a savior from your sins. Decide now and act.

PART FOUR

RELATIONSHIP HEALING

CHAPTER 9

Prodigal System of Forgiveness and Reconciliation

The parable of the prodigal son presents an excellent model for forgiveness and reconciliation. On the surface the parable does not appear to say much directly about forgiveness and reconciliation. In fact, it might appear from reading the parable that forgiveness and reconciliation are simple and just automatically happen. The younger son comes home and is immediately and graciously received by his father and given a party. This kind reception by the father gives the appearance that forgiveness and reconciliation is a simple emotional process. A little deeper and more thorough look at the parable, however, reveals that the father acted with thoughtful deliberation and not emotional impulsiveness.

If healing a relationship after a crisis were always easy, then the offender could simply pick up the phone and call and ask for forgiveness from the person he offended. The offended would instantly and automatically forgive him. Then the relationship between the two people would be reconciled, and the pair would resume a joyous, harmonious relationship, just like nothing had ever happened between them. But we know this is not how things work most of the time.

In reality, forgiveness and reconciliation are not simple because forgiveness and reconciliation are only a part of the larger process of healing the relational crisis. There are other components in this relational healing process besides forgiveness and reconciliation. For example, two others are remorse and restitution. When remorse and restitution are added to the healing equation, it becomes blatantly obvious that total healing is not going to be a simple process. No meaningful healing process is ever simple, straightforward, and automatic. It is hard work.

In APPENDIX B is a description of the background for the development of *The Prodigal System of Forgiveness and Reconciliation* model.

Forgiveness and reconciliation are actually separate processes. Sometimes people can forgive each other, but the offense was so devastating to one person that the relationship is not reconciled. Forgiveness does not automatically imply reconciliation. It takes only one person to forgive, but it takes two willing people to reconcile.

The offender and the offended each have their own individual process for forgiveness. Each person does this as an individual and separate from each other. For restitution, if the court system is not involved, both the offender and the offended work together toward a mutually agreeable restitution. For reconciliation, both the offender and the offended work together toward a mutually acceptable, reconciled relationship. Forgiveness must be completed by both the offender and the offended before the process of restitution and reconciliation can begin. Often restitution and reconciliation occur at the same time.

Restitution refers to the offender satisfactorily reimbursing the losses of the offended. The reimbursement the offender makes could be to pay back money taken, or it might be paying damages for destroyed or damaged property. Sometimes restitution compensates the offended for medical expenses or for emotional suffering. Sometimes restitution includes payment for damages or to defray expenses from lack of wages while a person recovers from a physical injury. Restitution is a complicated element in the healing process and is usually settled in the court system.

Reconciliation is not always possible or advisable. This part of relationship healing is always a difficult process. The difficulty stems from the fact that it takes two people to agree on the conditions of the reconciliation. Either person can halt the reconciliation process if his expectations of the other person are not being met. Reconciliation with an abusive person who has not sought treatment is not advisable. You have to use common sense regarding when it is safe to reconcile and when it is not a safe to reconcile a relationship.

There are many potential obstacles in the forgiveness and reconciliation process. These include such things as an unsatisfactory confession, insincere remorse, or inadequate restitution on the part of the offender. The anger of the offended can prevent forgiveness and quickly bring the reconciliation process to a halt. Many relationships are never rebuilt after a relational crisis. However many relationships are rebuilt. If you are in the process of healing a relational crisis, don't give up hope; but do expect to put in a lot of hard work to accomplish your goal of reconciliation.

The decision to forgive can be made by a person after being betrayed. Nothing is blocking the victim from forgiving the offender. Therefore, by itself, forgiveness is something anyone can achieve as part of his or her own personal healing process.

The offender is totally responsible for being remorseful. When the offender is truly remorseful, it makes the rest of the healing process easier. When the offender is not remorseful, the healing process usually cannot move forward. Still, the decision is controlled by the person offended.

It takes two people to accomplish the restitution and reconciliation part of the healing process, and it assumes that the offender has felt remorse. For restitution to take place, both the offender and the victim must agree on the proper restitution for the offense. If reconciliation is to take place, this also requires the agreement of the two people involved. For a relational crisis, it is necessary that both people desire reconciliation. When a crime is committed and the parties involved do not know each other, then reconciliation is probably not vital to the healing process in this instance.

Reconciliation is the making of peace between two people who make up and reestablish their friendship. Reconciliation is about two people who resolve their differences. When trust is involved in the reconciliation process, the two people usually agree that trust must be earned. The process of rebuilding trust requires the offender to meet certain criteria over a given period of time. Reconciliation typically requires the offender to accommodate the desires and needs of the offended.

Learning to forgive is the by-product of experiencing relational crises in our lives. Of course, some offenses are easier to forgive than others. For instance when the pain is from the loss of a little bit of money rather than personal abuse, this may be easier to forgive. The greater the intensity of the pain experienced, the harder it is to forgive the person who hurt us. However, once we understand forgiveness and know how to forgive, then forgiveness becomes an easier choice to make and practice. After years of practicing real forgiveness, it will become as natural and easy for us as it was for the father in the parable of the prodigal son.

Process of Forgiveness in a Relational Crisis

Phases in the Process

Chapter 2 lists the phases of healing from a relational crisis. The phases for forgiveness and reconciliation are the same as the phases of healing from a relational crisis. Going through the process of forgiveness and reconciliation is a crisis, so it makes sense that the phases are the same for forgiveness and reconciliation as for any other crisis. The phases are the same, but the content of each phase is different because each phase is addressing the same subject matter from a different point of view.

The phases in the process of forgiveness, restitution, and reconciliation are:

- Phase I is the Story/Drama/Consequences Phase
- Phase II is the Knowledge/Uncovering/Hope/Vision/Motivation Phase
- Phase III is the Decision/Choices/Belief Phase
- Phase IV is the Action/Change-of-Behavior Phase
- Phase V is the Deepening/Long-Term Proof/Wisdom-Maturity Phase
- Phase VI is the Restitution Phase
- Phase VII is the Reconciliation Phase

Forgiveness Principles

Forgiveness is unilateral, which means forgiveness depends on one person, the person who is hurt. In Jesus' parable, the father immediately forgave his younger son as soon as he left home with his inheritance. The father knew whom forgiveness was for. He also knew that the sooner he forgave, the better off he would be. So he forgave immediately.

Forgiveness depends only on the person wounded. Forgiveness is a choice the wounded person makes. The wounded person does it on his or her own timetable, and it does not depend at all on the perpetrator. Forgiveness does not depend on what the perpetrator does or says. Again, forgiveness is a choice that the wounded person makes when the time is right.

We all have heard "forgive and forget." But because we are humans, we cannot forget the facts of a crisis that we go through. We are never going to forget what happened to us. So "forgive and forget" does not work.

Forgiveness starts with a decision. You have to choose to forgive someone who hurt you. You also can choose not to forgive and hold onto the anger, resentment and bitterness you are feeling. You decide when to forgive when you want to release the anger, resentment, and bitterness you are holding.

When you forgive someone, it does not mean you have to reconcile with the offender. You never go back into an abusive relationship with someone who is violent.

Forgiveness does not mean you have to trust the offender. You do not make yourself vulnerable to someone who is not trustworthy. Trust must be earned by the offender. The offender has to prove his or her trustworthiness before you extend trust.

If you forgive someone, it does not mean you are excusing that person's behavior.

If you forgive someone, it does not mean you are pardoning the offender. You can forgive someone and still prosecute the person for the crime he or she has committed.

If you forgive someone, it does not mean you are letting the offender off the hook. The offender is still responsible for his or her bad choices and still has to deal with the consequences of his or her actions.

If you forgive someone, it does not mean you are indicating that the offense does not matter. When someone does not show you love and respect, it matters. You and your feelings matter. You are important, and you have the right to be treated with respect.

If you forgive someone, it does not mean you are condoning the offense. You are not saying it is OK that the person hurt you.

You do not have to confront someone in order to forgive the person. You may not know where the offender is, or you may not have access to the person, or the person who offended you could be dead. But you can forgive without being face to face with the person.

Forgiveness is for you. By not forgiving, you are holding onto anger, resentment, and bitterness. Someone has said that holding onto the anger, resentment, and bitterness is like drinking poison and hoping that the other person dies. Holding onto these negative emotions hurts you, and does not affect the offender at all. You are hurting yourself by not forgiving.

When you don't forgive, you are giving the offender the power to put your life into emotional turmoil whenever he or she wants to. You allow the offender to put you on an emotional rollercoaster by the things the offender says and does. In this situation, the offender can yank your chain anytime he or she wants to get you upset. Do you want this person to be in control of your emotions?

When you don't forgive, you are giving control of your life to the person you are focusing on. You think you have the control and the power, but you don't. The offender has control when you don't forgive. Do you want that person to be in control of your life?

In order to have the power over your own emotional and spiritual life, you will have to forgive your offender. The choice is yours. You forgive on your time frame. Since not forgiving hurts you, the sooner you forgive, the better off you will be. The sooner you forgive, the sooner you heal.

Process of Forgiveness for the Offended (Phases I – V)

The offender and the offended go through different processes in dealing with the same offense. First let's look at the process of forgiveness for the offended. Then we will look at the process that the offender goes through.

The Story/Drama/Consequences Phase (Phase I)

When offended, it is not unusual for a person to spend a lot of time thinking about, telling, and retelling the story of his hurt, suffering, or betrayal to anyone who will listen. The telling of the story is cathartic and healing. It is a very important part of the healing process.

In the cathartic process, the offended person talks about the effects the offense has had on his life.

The offended:

- verbalizes how he was hurt by the offender.
- tells how it makes him feel to have been treated when he was hurt or betrayed.
- tells how he is affected by being hurt.
- tells the consequences he and others are experiencing.
- tells how he has suffered because of the actions of the offender.

The offended often compares himself to the situation of the offender. He often feels additional resentment toward the offender because of the unfairness of the offense and how he is affected while the offender is able to go on with his life.

However, some people get stuck in the storytelling phase in some self-help groups. The person retells his story over and over again and remains a victim of his circumstances. The danger of doing this is that he becomes numb to his story. Each time he retells the story over a long period of time, he distances himself from the pain that occurred.

The healing begins with this catharsis in Phase I. But the catharsis of Phase I alone, even over a long period of time, does not heal the wounds. Catharsis is required in each phase to accomplish the purpose of the phase. Catharsis is moving thoughts into words, which ultimately results in choices being made to deal with the pain, with action and outward behaviors coming from these choices.

The Knowledge/Uncovering/Hope/Vision/Motivation Phase (Phase II)

This is the phase where the offended person becomes introspective about how he is handling being hurt. He acknowledges the anger, resentment, and bitterness he is harboring toward the offender. He starts realizing how harboring this anger and resentment is hurting himself and not affecting the offender. He notices that his family and friends are getting tired of hearing his story and that everyone is telling him to let it go and move on with his life. He also may notice that many people are beginning to avoid or ignore him and not return his phone calls.

It is not uncommon for the offended person to begin to not like the person he is becoming. He does not like himself as an angry bitter person. He may notice that he is becoming very short-tempered and has no patience with kids, friends, and family members. He can also become ashamed of his behavior towards family and friends. When shame is involved, he can start to believe that he is flawed and deserves what happened to him.

The offended may notice that he is becoming pessimistic and expects the worst to happen to himself in the future. He begins to view the world as a very unsafe and dangerous place to live. This can lead the person to feeling sad and hopeless, which can further lead to depression.

The misery in this phase motivates the person to seek solutions for change. The way out of this depression is forgiveness. Many people don't consider forgiveness until they are really miserable. Others wait until they are depressed and hopeless; these people usually require professional help to move out of this phase.

The Decision/Choices/Belief Phase (Phase III)

This is the phase where the offended makes the decisions about whether he is going to forgive and when he is going to forgive. The offended realizes that how he is handling things is not working and there must be a better way.

The offended person may read a book about the rewards of forgiveness. He may be convicted by recalling from his belief system the admonition to forgive. The offended may receive personal counseling and be confronted by his counselor to forgive in order to move on with his life. The offended realizes that he does have a choice to either stay like he is and remain miserable or change his attitude and forgive in order to move on and regain joy and happiness.

Forgiveness becomes an option, and the offended finally makes the choice and commitment to forgive his offender.

The Action/Change-of-Behavior Phase (Phase IV)

In this phase the offended person goes through the forgiveness exercise and verbally forgives the offender. After the act of forgiving, he may feel like a ton of bricks has been lifted off his shoulders. He feels relief from releasing all the negative emotions he has been carrying.

It may come as a surprise that a feeling of grief often follows forgiveness by the offended one. He is feeling the grief from the losses that came from the offense. He has to deal with these feelings by accepting the losses and letting go of the pain associated with them. This act of grieving can be a very painful process.

In is not unusual for the offended to feel empathy and compassion toward the person who hurt him. The offended begins to see that the offender probably was hurt in his past and is in need of personal healing from those childhood wounds.

The offended person now discovers within himself the capacity to love his offender with a nonjudgmental love, a godly love for a fellow human being dealing with his own set of problems and struggles.

The Deepening/Long-Term Proof/Wisdom-Maturity Phase (Phase V)

The offended's eyes are opened, and he sees other people struggling with hurts from circumstances similar to those he has been through. He sees that he is not alone in dealing with terrible and painful circumstances that life deals to people.

The offended one feels empathy for the people who are struggling and has the desire to help them deal with their pain. By helping others deal with struggles, he finds meaning in his own struggles and wants to share the healing.

The struggle that he dealt with provides a purpose and direction for his life. The event that took so much from him is now giving back to him something that is rewarding, meaningful, and significant. Not only is he changed on the inside, but his purpose in life is also changed.

Not many people desire to experience again the pain of a crisis. But most people prefer being the new person they have become because of experiencing the crisis.

Process of Forgiveness for the Offender (Phases I – V)

The Story/Drama/Consequences Phase (Phase I)

Most offenders keep quiet about their misbehaviors until caught. Then it is normal for the offender to spend a lot of time thinking about, telling, and retelling the story.

Often the con artist continually denies his involvement in a crime or betrayal and proclaims his innocence years after being convicted of a crime. Such individuals experience the consequences of their choices by spending months or years in jail or prison. We all know of these individuals. They begin to believe their own lies. Their hearts are hardened toward the truth.

There is another group of offenders who acknowledge their guilt and take responsibility for their misbehavior. Their deeds may or may not be crimes. Some of these people may also be convicted in the court system and serve time in the justice system for their crimes. But they take responsibility for their behavior.

The Knowledge/Uncovering/Hope/Vision/Motivation Phase (Phase II)

Here the offender begins to feel guilty and ashamed of his behavior, and he realizes that the guilt and shame he is feeling is hurting himself on the inside. He sees and acknowledges that his behavior and actions hurt the other person, and he feels remorse for what he had done to the other person.

The offender often begins to feel sorry for himself. He focuses on himself and the circumstances he has gotten himself into. He may see himself as becoming an extremely insensitive person with a cold heart toward others.

When he does not like the person he is becoming, then the healing process can begin. He acknowledges that the guilt and shame he is carrying is taking its emotional toll on him, and he is ready to deal with the guilt and shame he is feeling.

The Decision/Choices/Belief Phase (Phase III)

The offender makes the decision to seek forgiveness from the person he has offended. He is ready to get the burden of guilt lifted from his shoulders. He will do whatever it takes to get relief from the guilt. He truly desires to be free.

The Action/Change-of-Behavior Phase (Phase IV)

The offender confesses his misbehavior and injustice to the offended. He is able to acknowledge and verbalize his remorse for his actions.

The Deepening/Long-Term Proof/Wisdom-Maturity Phase (Phase V)

The offender agrees to help the offended heal the wounds and assist in the grief-healing process of the offended and the offended's family.

Restitution of the Offender to the Offended (Phase VI)

When a crime is committed, the restitution is often set by the court system. Otherwise, the offended and the offender must resolve the issue of restitution themselves. The offended states his expectations for restitution, and the offender states his intentions for restitution. The two people then negotiate a mutually agreeable settlement.

Reconciliation of the Offended and the Offender (Phase VII)

Forgiveness does not mean reconciliation. In most cases reconciliation is desirable, of course; but either person in a conflict can prevent reconciliation, and not all relationships should be reconciled. If a person is still dangerous, threatening, or abusive, then that person should not be allowed back into one's life.

A changed heart by the perpetrator warrants restoration and a chance to rebuild the relationship. After an offense, if the perpetrator is humbled, show compassion to him or her. After you forgive, you can remove the walls and be open and friendly toward the humbled offender.

The perpetrator's actions at this point will reveal the heart and character of the perpetrator. If the perpetrator wants to be reconciled, there are several things that need to take place. Acknowledging the incident demonstrates a changed heart. The perpetrator does not have to ask for forgiveness as part of the reconciliation process since the offended forgives as part of the restitution process, but the offender does need to acknowledge his wrongdoing. The offender expresses his feelings of not having any expectations of the person he wronged. He expresses what he feels he deserves from his bad behavior and places himself at the mercy of the person he hurt.

Bob (not his real name) came to one of the weekend workshops. He was forty years old and had recently assumed ownership of his family's home construction business when his father retired. Bob had always been a part of the business except for the years he was in college. Bob was very healthy and muscular from the manual labor he performed every day. The family business was doing well, and Bob was married to an attractive, outgoing woman. His son was about to graduate from high school and head to college on a baseball scholarship. Everything seemed perfect for Bob, but he had been struggling with depression for two years, and that was the reason he was attending our workshop.

During the weekend, Bob finally opened up about some things that happened to him when he was in high school and college. When he was fourteen, his unmarried aunt approached him about having sex. She was only six years older than he and the youngest of his mother's sisters. Bob gave in to the temptation and had sex with his aunt occasionally. He knew it was wrong and felt guilty the whole time he did it. During his college years, she occasionally came to see him, and they had sex. When Bob graduated from college, he married the daughter of a business associate. His wife was a Christian, and within a year after getting married, Bob became a Christian also. Bob now had been a Christian for twenty years and never told anyone about his past. Now the guilt and shame was taking its toll on him. Watching his own son go through his teen struggles brought back the memories he has suppressed all those years, and they tormented him night and day.

During the forgiveness segment of the workshop, Bob decided to forgive his aunt. We use role-playing in this segment of the workshop. So Bob stood in front of a woman who played the role of his aunt. Bob verbalized how she had hurt him and taken advantage of him. It was her fault. She tempted him, and it was too much for a young boy his age. It emotionally scarred him as he carried the guilt and shame for years. He felt dirty and like a second-class citizen. She was the cause of a lot of misery in his life. He had struggled with intimacy with his wife, and they had spent lots of time at the counselor's office working on marriage issues.

After Bob verbalized all this, he forgave her for everything she had done to him and all the misery she had caused him. He also forgave himself for his part. He also let go of the shame he was carrying. He had a tremendous load taken off his shoulders, and he was very grateful. He later called me and said he had seen his aunt and forgiven her to her face. She apologized for everything she had done and the pain she had caused him. They reconciled their friendship.

Self-Forgiveness

For most of us, forgiving ourselves is the hardest part in the healing process. It is easier to forgive someone for heinous crimes than to forgive ourselves for an insignificant lapse in judgment. We will forgive other people for something, but we will not forgive ourselves for the same thing. We are harder on ourselves than we are on other people. The following process is one that I have found works best for the majority of people.

The process begins with acknowledging your offense to God. Or to put it in biblical terms, you confess your sin to God. When you confess it to Him, He forgives you immediately and removes your guilt and shame. Now your fellowship with God is restored, and the Holy Spirit is again in control of your life.

Now is the time for you to forgive yourself. Acknowledge that you are only human and you make mistakes like every other human being. Acknowledge that God has forgiven you for this offense and removed your guilt and shame. If God can forgive you, then you can forgive yourself, right? Yes, you can. Go ahead and let yourself off the hook; forgive yourself.

Now that God has forgiven you, He wants you to forgive others just as He has forgiven you. You love Him and want to please Him since He by His grace has forgiven you much. He wants you to graciously forgive others. You forgive unilaterally, by your own choice, because forgiveness is for you, and it is a gift you are giving the person who hurt you. Freely you have received, freely give.

Also since God has forgiven you, you can go and ask forgiveness of anyone you have hurt. Acknowledge your fault, express your remorse, and make appropriate restitution.

If you are currently separated from your family or friends because of something you have done, consider going through the above process. You are only human and you make some lousy choices and hurt some people who love you. Can you acknowledge that you are human and not perfect? Can you acknowledge to God that you made some mistakes? Simply acknowledge your mistakes to Him, and He will forgive you. It is really that simple.

Yes, I know it is hard. You have been condemning and talking bad to yourself for a long time. You probably think you are a bad person and beyond hope. But that's a lie. There is hope for you. You can turn your life around. There is hope no matter what you have done.

Summary

The most important thing in life is relationships. When a relationship is broken, the healing process begins with forgiveness. For healing to take place, the offended must forgive his offender. The offender should acknowledge his offense to the offended and make the appropriate restitution. If both people so choose, the relationship can be reconciled. Usually the offender needs to forgive himself to complete the healing process.

Forgiveness is neither easy nor simple. Forgiveness is a process, sometimes a long and difficult one. Most people want to forgive but don't know how. Many people think they have forgiven when they really have not truly forgiven the person who offended them. Forgiveness brings healing to the body, mind, and soul. There is also a spiritual dimension to forgiveness. Learning to forgive is the best thing anyone can do. It has more rewards and benefits than any other life skill.

Do You Need to Forgive Someone?

If you are angry with someone, you are hurting yourself. You are the one suffering from your anger, not the person with whom you are angry. By holding on to anger, you are giving the other person control of your life. The other person is controlling your mood and attitude. The other person can send you into an emotional tailspin whenever he or she chooses to. Are you ready to get back control of your life? What are the anger, resentment, and bitterness doing to you? Are you happy about how this anger is affecting your relationship with God?

Ephesians 4:26 and 4:32 command us to deal with our anger and forgive: "Be angry, and yet do not sin; do not let the sun go down on your anger.... And be kind to one another, tender-hearted, forgiving each other, just as God in Christ also has forgiven you."

Matthew 6:14-15 reveals that God's forgiveness is directly related to our forgiveness of others: "For if you forgive men for their transgressions, our heavenly Father will also forgive you. But if you do not forgive men, then your Father will not forgive your transgressions."

Matthew 18:32-35 reveals the results of not forgiving: "You wicked slave, I forgave you all that debt because you entreated me. Should you not also have had mercy on your fellow slave, even as I had mercy on you? And his lord, moved with anger, handed him over to the torturers until he should repay all that was owed him. So shall My heavenly Father also do to you, if each of you does not forgive his brother from your heart."

Hebrews 10:30-31 reveals that vengeance is God's, not ours: "For we know Him who said, 'Vengeance is Mine, I will repay.' It is a terrifying thing to fall into the hands of the living God." Romans 12:17 and 19 reveal the same thing: "Never pay back evil for evil to anyone.... Never take your own revenge, beloved, but leave room for the wrath of God."

If you are still angry, you most likely want to strike out and hurt the person who hurt you so that he can suffer like you do. You want to take your own revenge. God says vengeance is His. By not forgiving, He is not forgiving you right now. The anger, resentment, and bitterness is eating you up. Are you ready to give this to God? Are you ready to let Him have the vengeance since it is His? Are you ready to have your prayers answered again? Are you ready to stop hurting yourself? Forgiveness is for you. Do it for yourself. Decide to forgive right now. Now forgive!

Are You an Offender and Currently in the Healing Process?

Psalm 31:9-10 reveals the inner struggle in the healing process: "I am in distress; my eye is wasted away from grief, my soul and my body also. For my life is spent with sorrow, and my years with sighing; my strength has failed because of my iniquity, and my body has wasted away.: Psalms 32:3-4 reveals the inner struggle of conviction: "When I kept silent about my sin, my body wasted away through my groaning all day long. For day and night Thy hand was heavy upon me; my vitality was drained away as with the fever-heat of summer."

Psalm 32:5 and verses 1-2 reveal the relief that comes from acknowledging sinful behavior: "I acknowledged my sin to Thee, and my iniquity I did not hide; I said, "I will confess my transgressions to the Lord" and Thou didst forgive the guilt of my sin. . . . How blessed is he whose transgression is forgiven, whose sin is covered. How blessed is the man to whom the Lord does not impute iniquity, and in whose spirit there is no deceit!"

If you are being eaten up inside with guilt, you need forgiveness for your offenses. Acknowledge your offense to the person you violated or wounded. Acknowledge your sin to God for your offense. Look at what the guilt is doing to you. Are you ready for relief and healing? An easy starting point is to confess all to God. He knows what you've done; it will not surprise Him when you acknowledge it to Him. Then acknowledge it to the person you wounded and reveal the remorse you are feeling. Then make appropriate restitution to the person. If possible, seek to reconcile the relationship. The rewards for this are great. Do it for your own healing. Just like the prodigal son, "come to yourself," and change your life. Decide now. You are worth it. Your life is worth it. You can change and become a new person. Your heart can be softened. Your life can have meaning. You can have a purpose. You can make a difference in the world. Plus you will sleep so much better. Decide now. Now act!

Are You Struggling with Forgiving Yourself?

You are not defined by your past. Just because you made poor decisions in the past does not mean you will make those same poor decisions in the future. You can come to yourself, decide to change yourself, and start making better decisions. The best decision to make right now is to follow the above process.

First, get God's forgiveness and forgive yourself. Then you can begin the process of healing the relationships you previously destroyed. You can change your circumstances. You can change yourself. There is hope. How? Once you acknowledge your sins to God, the Holy Spirit is there to give you the power and strength to change your path and yourself. There are lots of free resources for anyone who humbles himself, acknowledges he needs help, and commits to doing his part in turning his life around. Make the decision. Then act.

The younger son in the parable of the prodigal son was accepted back after his rebellious, prodigal adventure. This can be your story. Come to yourself; return to the family that loves you.

Foundations for *The Prodigal System of Forgiveness and Reconciliation* Model

Interpersonal forgiveness has its foundations in theology, philosophy, and psychology. The interpersonal forgiveness and reconciliation recovery program presented in this book is based upon both academic research and practical experience. From the academic community, this program is based on the therapeutic model and research produced at the University of Wisconsin-Madison by Robert Enright with the Human Development Study Group (1991, 1996, 2000) and on the Gayle Reed therapeutic model, which is an extrapolation from Enright's model. The Robert Enright and Gayle Reed forgiveness model is used in traditional counseling. The theological principles are taken from the Bible.

The Jim Carroll and David Bishop forgiveness model is used in intensive weekend workshops specializing in interpersonal forgiveness across the United States and Canada. Jim Carroll, David Bishop forgiveness model is used in **The Marriage Boot Camp** and **The Life Enrichment Boot Camp** workshops. (www. marriagebootcamp.com and www.lifeenrichmentbootcamps.com)

The Prodigal System of Forgiveness and Reconciliation is based on my practical experience in participating in over 125 workshops for adults and teenagers since 1998 under the mentoring of Jim

Carroll and David Bishop. *The Prodigal System of Forgiveness and Reconciliation* has been used in two workshops I developed: **The Experiential Divorce Recovery Workshop** and **The Teen Experiential Life Enrichment Workshop**. This book is the result of reworking and restructuring all of the above information and procedures into written material.

APPENDIX B

Phases in the *The Prodigal System of Forgiveness and Reconciliation* Model

- Phase I is the Story/Drama/Consequences Phase
- Phase II is the Knowledge/Uncovering/Hope/Vision/Motivation Phase
- Phase III is the Decision/Choices/Belief Phase
- Phase IV is the Action/Change-of-Behavior Phase
- Phase V is the Deepening/Long-Term Proof/Wisdom-Maturity Phase
- Phase VI is the Restitution Phase
- Phase VII is the Reconciliation Phase

LaVergne, TN USA
09 February 2010

172575LV00009B/404/P